Green Goddess

simple, quick and healthy recipes

ఇ

Raw/Cooked/Live – Vegan/Vegetarian – Suited for Diabetics

2nd edition

Sophia S Paul

ND, CYI, Author

Copyright © 2012 Sophia S Paul

All rights reserved.

ISBN-13:
978-1479146017

ISBN-10:
1479146013

www.royalyogabailey.com

www.amazon.com/author/sophiapaul

DEDICATION

This collection of recipes is dedicated to nature and the incredible abundance

she provides for all of us.

Thank you!

CONTENTS

    Note to the reader   i

1 **Introduction**   1

    Why and how to get started on Raw Food

    Going Shopping

    Ayurveda

2 **Tips to get Started**   13

    Why do I use –

    Celtic Sea Salt

    Sprouted Grain

    Seaweed

    Stevia

    Raw Cacao

3 **Recipes 26**

    1. **Green Juices and Smoothies 26**

Super Green Juices

    Other Smoothies and Juices

    Ruby Red Beet/Blueberry

    Coconut/Pineapple

    Banana/Cacao/Almond Butter

    Carrot/Apple/Ginger

    Carrot/Beet/Ginger

    2. **Breakfasts**   **39**

    Blue Corn/Berries Pancake

    Toasted Sprouted Grain w Fruit

    Oven baked Berry Pancake

    Peach/Cinnamon Waffles

    Baked Raspberry Pancake

    Apple/Blackberry/Vanilla Cobbler

    Coconut/Pineapple Breakfast Cake

    Permama's Oatmeal Cake

    Baked Cherry French Toast

    Vanilla gRAWnola

    Goji Berry/Cacao/Almond gRAWnola

3. **Salads 59**

   Roasted Choggia Beet/Peach/Kale Salad

   Raw Tuscan Kale Salad

   Sweet Potato/Black Bean Tortilla

   Black Bean/Red Rice/Sweet Potato

   Raw Lasagne

   Brown Quinoa/Tomato Salad

   Baked Roots

   Shredded Kale/Brussels's Sprouts Salad

   Sprouted Grain Veggie Wrap

   Cucumber/Kelp Noodle Salad

   Green/Verte/Gruen

4. **Cooked and Raw Dishes 76**

   Zucchini/Purple Potato Fritters

   Coconut/French Green Lentils/Bean Curry

   The Ultimate Veggie Wrap

   Avocado/Nori Rolls

   Nori Rolls and Red Lentil Salad

   Chipotle Chili

   Sweet Potato Burgers

   Alfalfa/Nori/Avocado Sandwich

   Green Lentil/Asparagus Soup

   Broccoli/Avocado/Quinoa Warm Salad

Mushroom/Sundried Tomato Quiche

5. **Appetizers 97**

    Savory Blue Corn Waffles

    Vegan Cheeses

    Walnut/Rosemary Pate

    Grape Tomato/Basil Appetizer

    Artichoke Spread

    Lavender/Sea Salt Roasted Almonds

6. **Cookies and Desserts 105**

    Frozen Vegan Almond Butter Dessert

    Chocolate/Fruit Bars

    Chocolate/Almond Bars

    Banana/Oatmeal/Cacao Nibs Cookies

    Raw Cookies

    Coconut Milk/Chocolate Mousse

    Gotta Have Them Now Cookies

    Dark Chocolate Cake

    Peach Pie

    Peach Pie Raw Version

7. **Salsas 120**

    Mango/Black Bean/Roasted Corn Salsa

    Peach/Tomato/Roasted Corn Salsa

    Green Lentil/Black Bean/Tomato Salsa

    Grilled Corn/Black Bean/Peach Salsa

8. **Beverages 126**

   Iced Rosemary Tea

   Iced Ginger Tea

   White Wine Spritzer

   Fruit Water

9. **Fermented Food 129**

   Fermented Cabbage

   Kimchi

Final Thoughts and Food for Thought 133

- Goddess Tara

Recommended Reading

About the Author

*The greatest delight the fields and woods minister is the suggestion of an occult relation
between man and the vegetable. I am not alone and unacknowledged.
They nod to me and I to them.*
~Ralph Waldo Emerson

ಐ

note to the reader

I am glad your path has led you to "Green Goddess". The simple fact that your journey directed you here and our paths crossed is a sign that your soul is telling you to take a look at other possibilities, to open yourself up to living a healthier, happier, greener life.

Sophia S Paul

what this book is and isn't

It is NOT a nutritional book nor is it meant to give medical advice. It IS a fun and creative tool to help you to try some healthy alternatives that will greatly improve your life and well-being. All recipes are developed, tried and used many times by the author. They are easy and quick to prepare. They all are meant as an inspiration – be creative, substitute with whatever is in season, looks fresh and good to you or even adjust to what you grow in your own garden or on your window sill. There are no limitations to what you can do with this. Most of all have fun!!

This book contains a collection of recipes that I have developed over many years. Please use the blank space in each chapter to capture your notes, thoughts, ideas and possible changes and additions to each recipe.

I am sending you blessings of abundance, health and happiness through each and every recipe in my book. Enjoy and share with likeminded souls (and stomachs) and maybe you can help someone else on their own path to a healthier life.

Please visit my website www.royalyogabailey.com, scroll through the pages, utilize what resonates with you and if you need any additional help please contact me about my Natural Health Consultations; a link can also be found on my website.

1 ~ introduction

It's difficult to think anything but pleasant thoughts while eating a homegrown tomato.
~Lewis Grizzard

green – raw – vegan – vegetarian….

…sugar free, low carb, no processed foods…. Oh, oh. Will any of these recipes even taste ok?

Believe me, they are delicious!!! AND you will feel so much better, you will get "the" GLOW!!! Your energy will increase dramatically, aches and pains disappear, pounds will drop almost miraculously and those allergies… what allergies you may ask in a few weeks after following my suggestions!

Your new path will be a very healing and even a spiritual experience when done correctly. Take it slow and at your own pace. Be patient but consistent and most of all have fun and experiment. Substitute ingredients for what is fresh and in season or is more of your personal preference (as long as it is in line with your healthy goals of course).

Over many years of living, eating and teaching GREEN I have witnessed in myself as well as in my family and clients what profound changes and healing can occur through some simple but consistent changes towards a healthier, greener lifestyle. GREEN doesn't necessarily mean all you eat is just spinach, broccoli and lettuce. GREEN means healthy, clean and pure!!! Some of the recipes in this book are delicious breakfasts, cakes and desserts that contain chocolate (raw), almonds and nuts. There are wraps made with sprouted grain or nori sheets. There are some cooked foods, combined with raw ingredients and juices that include lots of tasty fruit. No worries, I am not going to make you an extremist! Why? Because I don't believe in being fanatic. But I do believe in healthy eating and how it can help you feel and look the best you can!

Take it slow, eliminate what is easiest for you first, for me it was sugar and white flour, then pork, then came red meat. After reading the "World Peace Diet" chicken never saw my kitchen or stomach again. Dairy went next, to be followed by fish and seafood.. Now I am eating less and less grain products as well and if I do I prefer sprouted grains.

The entire process took me many years and it was a very natural path. I just became more and more aware of how food is processed, handled and treated. I did not want to be part of a "killing and torture mentality" anymore. And eating flesh foods or any animal products (except eggs occasionally) is just that. My eggs are from free ranging chickens, fed with organic grain and gathered by my grandkids – just imagine the great energy THEY carry. But I still don't eat very many.

Part of the process of course is my yogic lifestyle, my passion for yoga and meditation and that includes no killing and harming - Ahimsa, in Sanskrit, one of the yogic rules of living also called the yamas/niyamas.

Did I mention that I have been a diabetic for many years? Certainly that contributed to my food and lifestyle choices. Per my doctor I am managing the diabetes perfectly well with just diet. I don't need insulin nor any other prescription drugs. I do take some supplements though. But my food is my medicine – just as it should be.

However, everybody is different and I advise you to please make sure to consult your (Alternative) Health Care Provider if you have any medical condition and let them know about your plan.

why and how to get started on raw food

I would like to take a moment to talk a little about raw food and how to slowly transition from our current diet to a raw food diet. I am not 100% raw but I eat as much raw as I can and I always trust my body and what it needs. On cold days – that we have very often here at 9000 feet in the Colorado Mountains – my body is telling me that I need something to warm me up. It is possible to just warm your raw soup/food to 115 degrees to preserve the enzymes, but sometimes it is so cold that all I want is some hot food, and I mean hot! That is ok; it makes my body feel better and still can be a very healthy choice. In the summer though I hardly ever turn on the stove.

The raw food diet is not a new fad but was actually promoted over 30 years ago by Dr Max Gerson, then continued by his daughter Charlotte Gerson. It was discovered that by introducing raw foods (mainly in the form of raw juices) they were able to heal terminally ill people.

"How do I become Raw?"

1. First, we don't need to be 100% Raw to be healthy.

One can be very healthy during a transition without 100% Raw Food Diet. It takes a while and the unhealthier our habits were the slower we want to take the transition.

It is critically important to understand that what we leave out of our diet completely is the way to ultimate health. What we *don't* eat is actually more important than what we *do* eat.

So what do we need to eliminate? Here goes: sugar, white flour, all flesh foods, dairy, processed foods, transfats. There are so many healthy alternatives as you will find out throughout this book that there is no need for harmful food to be eaten. Even if you decide to never become a 100% raw foodist you will still reap tremendous benefits just by making one small healthy change at a time.

2. What are the benefits?

The reason a 100% Raw Food Diet is the greatest diet in the world is because we leave out everything that could make us ill and only keep in the best of foods. The key to healing is to restore the mostly acid body to an alkaline environment.

3. There are certain foods that we all know are detrimental to perfect health:
- ❖ Animal Protein
- ❖ Dairy
- ❖ Refined Sugar – Cake, Cookies, Candy, Bakery items
- ❖ Processed Starches – Bread, Pasta, Cereal

These are the ones we need to eliminate first.

4. What do we want to eat:
- ❖ Raw Vegan Foods – Vegetables, Fruits, Nuts, Seeds, and Sprouts

With a raw food diet one will be able to gently and thoroughly detoxify the body (only with wise raw food choices such as green juices, smoothies, raw salads); it is amazing how easy it is to lose extra pounds AND have incredible energy.

Green juices lower your pH from a more acidic to a more alkaline state; therefore promoting a reduction of inflammation which is the cause of many illnesses.

"Your situation is not hopeless and you are not helpless. No one food supplement or medication can solve anyone's medical problem, ever. The body has natural remedial capabilities to heal itself, once you leave out the cause of disease. Diet is the key. What you leave out of your diet completely is what heals you. Supplements are a great addition to a better diet" says Matt Monarch.

With a raw food diet our bodies will slowly and naturally start to detoxify. I find it important to take it slow so that your body can adjust to the new healthy food in a natural way. It will also take your taste buds a while to accept and eventually LOVE the new food choices you are making. If you are going too fast you may go through withdrawal and get frustrated. I suggest to replace one unhealthy food/habit a day or even per week with a healthy one.

Regardless of how fast or slow you proceed you could experience some detox symptoms that may appear as a cold or flu, with runny nose, weakness/sleepiness, diarrhea and so forth. If it lasts just for a short time be assured that this is a good sign. Of course if it lasts longer than 2 or 3 days you might want to consult with your health practitioner.

The more raw and health food you eat your body will become pure and clean again; your immune system has a chance to heal, inflammation will be reduced and your overall health will improve dramatically.

The longer you are raw or partially raw, the more sensitive you become. Processed foods you ate before, are no longer tolerated.

Even if we eat completely healthy, waste still accumulates in our cells and tissues from sources such as environmental toxins, residue from food, adrenalin from nervous tension, fear, and stress, and dead cells that are produced all the time.

It is important to keep up our healthy habits not only about the food we eat but also what kind of cleaning products, shampoos and body washes we use as well as keeping our thoughts and emotions clean.

If you would like more detailed information I highly recommend the following books:
1. Charlotte Gerson with Beata Bishop: Healing the Gerson Way (Carmel, CA: Totality Books, 2009).
2. Ann Wigmore: The Hippocrates Diet and Health Program focuses on the same principles.

More recent authorities on "Green Live Food" are
1. Will Tuttle, PhD: The World Peace Diet (Lantern Books)
2. Gabriel Cousens, M.D. (Rainbow Green Live-Food Cuisine; There is a Cure for Diabetes)
3. David Wolffe (The Sunfood Diet Success System)

something important to consider when you go shopping

According to EWG (Environmental Working Group), the most polluted fruits and vegetables are:

- Apples
- Celery
- Sweet bell peppers
- Peaches
- Strawberries
- Nectarines
- Grapes
- Spinach
- Lettuce
- Cucumbers
- Blueberries
- Potatoes

EWG recommends to buy only organic fruits and vegetables included in this list of highly polluted fruits and veggies. On the other side, EWG has elaborated a list of fruits and veggies low in pesticides including:

- Onions
- Sweet Corn
- Pineapples
- Avocado
- Cabbage
- Sweet peas
- Asparagus
- Mangoes
- Eggplant
- Kiwi
- Cantaloupe

- Sweet potatoes
- Grapefruit
- Watermelon
- Mushrooms

thoughts on ayurveda

Ayurveda is considered the sister science of yoga and based on my experience as a long-term yogini I need to at least mention some of the benefits of the ayurvedic lifestyle here. Of course I am limiting this to the food part since this is not a book about Ayurveda per se.

Ayurveda identifies 6 tastes by which all foods can be categorized: Sweet, Sour, Salty, Bitter, Pungent, and Astringent. The first four tastes are relatively easy to recognize, the last two may not seem familiar. Pungent taste is hot and spicy as found in a chili pepper, while the astringent taste is dry and light as found in popcorn.

Ayurveda suggest to incorporate all six tastes in each meal. Below is a chart that gives an overview of the qualities according to your dosha.

The most balancing are:

Vata   Sweet, Sour, Salty

Pitta   Sweet, Bitter, Astringent

Kapha   Pungent, Bitter, Astringent

The most aggravating are:

Vata   Bitter, Pungent, Astringent

Pitta   Sour, Salty, Pungent

Kapha Sweet, Sour, Salty

Ayurveda is based on the principles of three doshas. Doshas are the energies that make up every individual, which perform different physiological functions in the body and can be wonderfully balanced through ayurvedic lifestyle, Yoga and Meditation.

Here is a very brief overview of the 3 Dosha types:

1. Vata Dosha -- Energy that controls bodily functions associated with motion, including blood circulation, breathing, blinking, and your heartbeat.

In balance: There is creativity and vitality.
Out of balance: Can produce fear and anxiety.

2. Pitta Dosha -- Energy that controls the body's metabolic systems, including digestion, absorption, nutrition, and your body's temperature.

In balance: Leads to contentment and intelligence.
Out of balance: Can cause ulcers and anger.

3. Kapha Dosha -- Energy that controls growth in the body. It supplies water to all body parts, moisturizes the skin, and maintains the immune system.

In balance: Expressed as love and forgiveness.
Out of balance: Can lead to insecurity and envy.

It is said that when all three doshas are balanced we are able to attain the perfect state of health. To bring us back to the food part here is a short description of what the tastes mean:

Sweet taste results from the combination of water and earth and is heavy, moist, and cooling by nature. In Ayurveda however sweet is not associated with sugary foods as it is commonly associated with this taste here in the West. Sweet taste is also found in milk (where in the case of this book of course we are talking almond/coconut/hemp/rice/oat milk), most grains (especially wheat, rice, and barley), many legumes (like beans and lentils), sweet fruits (such as bananas and mangos), and certain cooked vegetables (such as carrots, sweet potatoes, and beets).

Sweet taste naturally increases bulk, moisture, and weight in the body; it is excellent for supporting and nourishing blood, fat, muscles, bones, marrow, and reproductive fluids. Sweet taste also increases saliva, soothes mucous membranes and burning sensations, relieves thirst, and has beneficial effects on the skin, hair, and voice.

Sour Taste is composed of earth and fire and has the qualities of hot, light, and moist. It is commonly found in citrus fruits (such as lemon and limes), and fermented constituents (including wine, vinegar, pickles, sauerkraut, and soy sauce). Sour taste stimulates digestion, helps circulation and elimination, energizes the body, strengthens the heart, relieves thirst, maintains acidity, sharpens the senses, and helps extract minerals such as iron from food. It also nourishes all the vital tissues except the reproductive tissues.

Salty taste is composed of fire and water and is hot, heavy, and is considered moist. We find it in any salt (such as sea salt and rock salt), sea vegetables (like seaweed and kelp). It has a drying quality in the mouth. In moderation, salty taste improves the flavor of food, improves digestion, lubricates tissues, liquefies mucous, maintains mineral balance, aids in the elimination of wastes, and calms the nerves. Since it has the tendency to attract water, it also improves the radiance of the skin.

Pungent is related to the elements of fire and air. It is hot, dry, and light. It is found in vegetables such as chili peppers, garlic, and onions, as well as in spices such as black pepper, ginger, and cayenne. In small amounts, pungent taste stimulates digestion, clears the sinuses, promotes sweating and detoxification, dispels gas, aids circulation, improves metabolism, and relieves muscle pain.

Bitter taste has the nature of air and ether and is light, cooling, and dry. We find it in green leafy vegetables such as spinach, kale, and green cabbage and other vegetables like zucchini and eggplant. Certain herbs and spices (turmeric, fenugreek, and dandelion root), coffee, tea, and fruits such as grapefruits, olives, and bitter melon. Bitter taste stimulates the appetite and helps bring out the flavor of the other tastes. It is also a powerful detoxifying agent, and has antibiotic, anti-parasitic, and antiseptic qualities. It helps with skin rashes, water retention, fever, burning sensations and nausea as well as supporting weight loss.

Astringent taste resembles the combination of air and earth. It is dry, cooling, and heavy and can be found in legumes (such as beans and lentils), fruits (including cranberries, pomegranates, pears, and dried fruit), vegetables (such as, broccoli, cauliflower, artichoke, asparagus and turnip), grains (such as rye, buckwheat, and quinoa), spices and herbs (including turmeric and marjoram), coffee, and tea. Astringent taste has a cooling effect on the body as well.

For further reading I recommend
1. Ayurvedic Healing by David Frawley
2. Textbook of Ayurveda by Dr Vasant Lad

there's magic in a green lifestyle!

There's magic in a GREEN lifestyle! And it doesn't necessarily mean "green" for the color. With GREEN I mean "healthy, vibrant, clean, pure life/live food", food that nourishes and heals and gives you boundless energy, a youthful appearance and a vivacious glow.

And YOU are about to discover what that magic can do for YOU!!!

And now

Let's get started!!!

2 ⚘ tips to get started

Shipping is a terrible thing to do to vegetables.
They probably get jet-lagged, just like people.
~Elizabeth Berry

This one of my favorite photographs, you have seen it on the cover and the back of the book.

It is a picture that I took just recently in my greenhouse. Nothing can look healthier and/or greener than this, wouldn't you agree?

- ❖ important information:

  - ❖ Eggs can always be substituted with the equal amount of soaked chia seeds or ground and soaked flax seeds.
  - ❖ Please use as much organic product/produce as you can
  - ❖ During the summer of course I harvest most of my food from my own land and greenhouses
  - ❖ I suggest you start gardening as well, even if you live in an apartment you could start an herb garden on your window sill; if you happen to have a porch or balcony, consider container gardening! Nothing is more rewarding, grounding and inspiring as growing, harvesting and eating your own home grown food!!!
  - ❖ Most of what I need to buy I get from a place like Vitamin Cottage (locally here in the Denver area); during the winter months I get deliveries (very reasonable) from a local food coop (www.doortodoororganics.com) ; anything else I can order online from companies like vitacost.com and others. Do a little research on your own and if you find something interesting and reasonable please let me know – I am always interested in checking out new sources.
  - ❖ I do not use nor do I own a microwave!!!! That is the first piece of equipment to toss out. Even if not in use it emits harmful microwaves; when used to heat or cook food the food is rendered useless at the cellular level; nutrients are destroyed, your body cannot absorb any of it, all vitamins, nutrients, minerals are dead.
  - ❖ In the long run you might want to invest into a dehydrator, but to start with it is not necessary. Just see how you feel and if you stick with the program, pick the easier recipes first and proceed from there.
  - ❖ You will need a high power blender though. As always I try to go with inexpensive options: I am using a blendtec product. Works well enough for me. But if you want to go fancy, get a more expensive, even more powerful one. There are plenty of those on the market.

- ❖ I highly suggest a water filter. I am using a water alkilizer which is currently the best you can find on the market. The water tastes delicious, bacteria, viruses and such are removed up to 99.99% and your body is able to absorb this super clean water much better.

- ❖ I am slowly getting rid of all plastic utensils, storage containers and bowls in my kitchen, too many harmful chemicals can leach out of them and into my food. I just purchased an inexpensive citrus press made from glass; for my coffee (yes, I am still drinking –organic- coffee) I use an old fashioned ceramic coffee filter (tossed out the coffee maker that pours hot water into the plastic filter… guess what leaches into the coffee that way….). My mixing bowls are ceramic, glass or stainless steel. My cook pots are all slowly replaced with stainless steel or those with a ceramic coating. No, I did not do this all at once, it was a long process and is still a work in progress.

- ❖ As for spatulas, scrapers, spoons and such I am using bamboo or stainless steel as much as possible.

- ❖ Unfortunately I haven't found an alternative for my cuisine art food processor as the bowl is made from plastic, but as soon as it is time for replacement in comes the one with the stainless steel bowl!!

- ❖ On another note and a more spiritual level I like to bless my food. It all starts already when I plant my garden. I can't help it but it always makes me happy and puts me in a good mood when I work in the garden. I think my plants notice that and the good energy and blessings transfer into them. That then continues when I care for them, water them, feed them, and finally harvest them, with gratitude and love in my heart; with the awareness of the abundance and nourishment I bring the harvest into my kitchen. And once again, preparing the food while I think positive thoughts, sometimes chanting or humming the blessings and prayers are potentiated. How can food not be nourishing and healthful when grown, harvested and prepared in a sacred manner.

- ❖ Even food that needs to be bought and supplemented can be changed on an energetic level by blessing it – if you are familiar with the ancient healing modality of Reiki you can reiki your food by thinking or drawing the reiki symbols over the food. (for local Reiki classes please contact me)

Every recipe will be marked as follows:

R = Raw

C = Cooked

V = Vegan

Veg = Vegetarian (the addition "ovo" means eggs, "lacto" means dairy, however the only dairy product that is mentioned here is butter and can easily be substituted with coconut oil)

D = (suited for) Diabetics

Here is what you will see throughout the book:

R, C, V, Veg, D

why do I use:

❖ Why Celtic Sea Salt?

Sea salt is often marketed as the healthier, more natural alternative to regular table salt. Sea salt is produced through the evaporation of seawater, which leaves behind some trace minerals and elements depending on its water source. Although most sea salts have a pink or gray hue, a coarse appearance and a subtle flavor, there are differences in nutritional content that cannot be seen with the naked eye. Celtic sea salt, in particular, has acquired recognition beyond other salts due to its unique nutritional makeup.

By Carla Delangre:

Salt tends to be a topic of common misconceptions. With so many varieties it is difficult for consumers to decide on which to purchase. The basic knowledge of salt starts with an understanding of table salt versus sea salt.

Table Salt was formulated in the early 1900s. During the Great Depression when goiters were becoming an issue across mass population due to iodine deficiencies, iodine was added. Morton Salt became the first company to add both iodine and dextrose to its standard table salt in 1924, the dextrose acting as a stabilizer.

The salt came from the pacific coast and the Great Lakes where they wash and process the salt, leaching it of any trace minerals. Adopting from the Swiss practices the US government added sodium iodide and potassium iodide to the salt, which turned the salt purple. They couldn't sell purple salt, so they bleached it to bring it to a more favorable color. The bleach caused a bitter flavor so dextrose was added to sweeten the salt and to stabilize the iodide. The Dextrose then caused a sticky texture, which inhibited an easy pour use, so anti-caking chemicals were added create free flowing table salt. So, in the end you are left with 99.9% sodium chloride along with unnatural chemicals.

The body must assimilate sodium and chloride with potassium element bondage. Sodium is essential for proper absorption of other major nutrients and functioning of nerves and muscles, and also necessary for hydration throughout the body.

There are two types of sea salt, mined and ocean. All sea salt originally came from the ocean. Mined sea salts come from ancient sea beds that form over an extended period of time and form into a rock material.

Ocean salt comes fresh from the ocean and is harvested by hand. Using various methods including salt flats. The salt flats are shallow clay or silica lined beds that have water from the ocean flowing into. With the assistance of sunshine and wind, the water and salt separate and crystalize. The delicate crystals are then raked by hand into piles where farmers harvest and deliver to a coop. Celtic Sea Salt® is a 35 year old brand of salt that is sustainably harvested from origins all over the world. The sources are handpicked and scientifically analyzed for mineral content and to ensure no pollutants or contaminants are present in the harvest. The natural occurring mineral balance allows the body to assimilate sodium, and is naturally lower in sodium and chloride. Each day we lose sodium through sweat, tears and other excretions, which causes a need for daily, replenish of sodium. Celtic Sea Salt® is Doctor recommended from practitioners all over the world due to the perfect mineral balance.

Celtic Sea Salt® is offered in many user-friendly varieties. The Light Grey is perfect for cooking as it dissolves well in heat and liquids. The fine ground is a wonderful consistency for baking. And the Flower of the Ocean® is a delicate crystal that crushes easily between your fingers to finish any dish.

Once you have experienced the full flavor of moist, mineral rich Celtic Sea Salt®, in comparison to processed salt, you will find that all your meals taste incredibly better using whole sea salt. Now you have found the secret ingredient to making all dishes better. Over time your pallet will be seasoned to tasting the subtle differences of whole salts from around the world, similar to wine or cheese connoisseur pallets. Enjoy what nature has given us, salt of the earth.

Recommended Reading

Dr. David Brownstein, Salt Your Way to Health

Jacque Delangre, Sea Salt's Hidden Powers

About the Author of this article:

Carla Delangre is the granddaughter of Jacque Delangre who founded the Celtic Sea Salt® brand. She has traveled all over the world with her family studying many sea salt sources and has been educated by the many doctors who recommend the Celtic Sea Salt® brand. Once she finished her Holistic Culinary training she has joined her family in the sea salt business to continue her grandfather's legacy.

"This (Celtic Sea Salt® Brand) is the one I use. It has a long track record with me. This is what I recommend for my patients." - Dr. David Brownstein, M.D. and Board-Certified Family Physician who utilizes the best of conventional and alternative therapies. He is the Medical Director for the Center for Holistic Medicine in West Bloomfield, Michigan.

"I've enjoyed using Celtic Sea Salt® for several years now. It enhances the flavor of whole foods and provides me and my family with a superior source of trace minerals." - Christiane Northrup, M.D. Author of Women's Wisdom

"Many illnesses are caused or exacerbated by trace-mineral deficiencies. These can be avoided by the liberal use of Celtic Sea Salt® in your cooking and the complete avoidance of all other salts, all of which contain only pure sodium chloride." - Thomas S. Cowan, M.D.

❖ Why is Sprouted Grain better for you?

Food For Life breads (the Ezekiel brand that I am referring to in my recipes) are flourless. They utilize only fresh sprouts as the sole base of their bread dough – without flour. A few bullet points are:

1. Sprouts become more nutrient rich after germination through enzymatic activity.

2. Enzymes found in the bran and germ break down phytic acid (an absorption inhibitor found in grains such as wheat) which promotes digestibility.

3. Sprouted grains become lower glycemic than the grains from which they were sprouted, because the starch found in the endosperm is converted into maltose.

4. Sprouting grains alkalizes them to a more neutral ph level

Sprouted grains provide more protein, vitamins and minerals than refined flours, there are biochemical changes taking place during germination that increase the accessibility of vitamins, proteins and carbohydrates.

Grains attain their densest nutrition during their sprouts' germination. Water-soaked wheat berries germinate in two to three days, and as their little white shoots grow, enzymes and chemicals break down the seed and prepare the wheat's germ and endosperm to nourish the growing plant. This germination enhances the availability of vitamins A, B and C; releases the elements iron, potassium and calcium; and markedly elevates protein levels. Herbs are Special's wheat commentary states that after three days wheat sprouts' protein and vitamin contents can have increased 300 to 600 percent.

Besides increasing the grains protein and vitamins, germinated sprouts contribute carbohydrates that are easier for you to digest because their starches have already been broken down by enzymes. This reductive action in the presence of high protein and fiber levels does not necessarily lead to tough sprouts or dense loaves; the sprouts are slowly ground when being made into dough. If you are diabetic, sprouted wheat bread has a low glycemic index and does not cause post-meal blood-sugar levels or blood-fat counts to spike upwards. If you are reducing calories, sprouted wheat breads provide, ounce-for-ounce, more protein and nutrition than many pre-packaged, highly-processed "diet foods." If you are vegetarian, sprouted bread can accompany any meal, toasted, baked, fried, grilled, cubed for stuffing, mashed for pudding or stretched for pizza. If you are pregnant, sprouted wheat bread, being easily digested and nutrient-dense, is likely to support your health as well as normal fetal development, because it has increased nutrient content, and yet retains important folic acid found in the original grain, which can be lost during the milling of grain into flour process.

And here is a statement from Food For Life:

Food For Life Baking Co. is located in Corona, California. Since our inception over 50 years ago, we've been serving the health conscious consumer with natural baked goods made from only the finest natural ingredients.

At Food For Life, we believe simple is better - in all our baked goods. We believe if you can't pick it or pluck it, we don't want it in our breads. So we go to great lengths to make better products from the best natural ingredients possible. Food For Life, offers a complete line of flourless, sprouted grain, certified organic baked goods including Ezekiel 4:9 and Genesis 1:29 product lines. You can choose from sprouted grain breads, English muffins, tortillas, buns, cereal and pasta. Why sprouted you ask? Because, sprouting promotes digestibility and increases nutrition, which makes great sense to include in your diet. And, it also makes several Food For Life products low glycemic and diabetic friendly. We also offer a complete line of gluten free and vegan breads, tortillas, and new English muffins.

With just one bite, you'll know they're a Food For Life. Visit us at foodforlife.com

❖ What are the benefits of seaweed?

For some people, seaweed is a much-loved plant food used in soups, salads, side dishes and as a condiment or sushi wrapper. For others, it's an acquired taste. Some of the most popular edible seaweeds include deep green kombu, dried black hijiki, chewy red dulse, emerald wakame, bright, leafy sea lettuce, and dark, toasted nori.
Although each is a unique food, with distinctive taste and texture, all of these "sea vegetables" are valuable sources of nutrients with many of the same health benefits as land vegetables.

Source of Nutrients

Most seaweeds are high in essential amino acids, which makes them valuable sources of vegetable protein in a vegetarian or mostly meatless diet.

Like most land vegetables, seaweeds contain vitamins A (beta carotene) and C. Seaweeds are rich in potassium, iron, calcium, iodine and magnesium because these minerals are concentrated in sea water. They are also one of the few vegetable sources of vitamin B-12.

Weight Control

Seaweed is a "free food" when it comes to weight control because it provides only 5 to 20 calories in a serving and contains virtually no fat. Its fiber content also contributes to a feeling of satiety, or fullness when eaten in a meal.

Japanese researchers at Hokkaido University have discovered that a substance in brown seaweeds called fucoxanthin helps reduce the accumulation of fat in the body cells of laboratory animals--although there is no evidence that these results carry over to humans.

Salt Substitute

Seaweed granules have been tested in the United Kingdom as a flavor enhancer that could replace sodium in snack foods and other processed food products. Cutting back on salt can reduce the risk of high blood pressure, which reduces the risk of heart attack or stroke.

Blood Sugar Regulation

When eaten as part of a meal, seaweed can help balance blood sugar because its soluble fiber content helps slow the rate at which foods are digested and absorbed into the bloodstream.

Digestive Aid

Agar agar is a gelling agent made from seaweed that's high in soluble fiber. When used as a laxative, agar agar soaks up water in the intestine and swells up. This creates movement in the bowels that helps with elimination of waste.

Other Possible Benefits

Seaweed extracts have been shown to have an anti-cancer and anti-inflammatory effect on laboratory animals, though this has not been scientifically proven in humans.

by Molly McAdams

- ❖ What is Stevia?

Stevia rebaudiana (Bertoni) is a South American plant native to Paraguay that traditionally has been used to sweeten beverages and make tea. The word "stevia" refers to the entire plant and its components, only some of which are sweet. The sweet tasting components of the stevia plant are called steviol glycosides. Steviol glycosides can be isolated and purified from the leaves of the stevia plant and are now added to some foods, beverages and tabletop sweeteners in the U.S. and elsewhere.

(http://www.steviabenefits.org/)

- ❖ What you need to know about Raw Cacao

Raw cacao powder is created by processing raw cacao beans through a cold-pressing process with the cacao fat removed. All raw forms of cacao are said to be powerhouses of iron, dietary fiber, calcium, zinc, potassium and antioxidants.

Raw cacao is said to promote the release of neurotransmitters, which promote a positive outlook and bodily rejuvenation, and release feel-good hormones.

Raw cacao/cacao nibs are rich sources of antioxidant flavonoids that promote cardiovascular health and protect against toxins. The antioxidant flavonoids in raw cacao can help improve circulation, regular heartbeat and blood pressure. Additionally, they help the body repair itself and resist free-radical toxins.

adapted from www.livestrong.com

However – Jennifer Murray (Vegetarian Food) believes that "raw cacao is just like most things in the world of health and nutrition- the information changes fast. You need to keep on top of the news. There are many that believe that chocolate, even in its purest form of raw cacao, is still not very good for you, perhaps even toxic. The stimulant quality may agitate kidney and liver functioning. Some tests find it to be addictive, leading to mood swings and other withdrawal symptoms when not consumed regularly. Sexual dysfunction has also been listed as a possible side effect of chocolate intake- yikes! Certainly you must never blindly trust the information given to you by someone who is selling the product. Conduct your own research and see what the experts are saying. Though chocolate may not be the knight in shining armor that so many of us wish it was, when eaten in moderation, it doesn't seem to be causing too much harm either. To play it safe, consume chocolate on special occasions and look for your magnesium and antioxidants elsewhere."

I would like to add as my dad used to say "Like everything else in life – moderation is key".

3 ~ recipes

1 green juices and smoothies

> A word of caution first for diabetics. Please check with your health care provider and monitor your blood sugar carefully, as some juices and smoothies can raise glucose levels. Dr. Esselstyn states "Drinking smoothies will elevate blood sugar — and for some people this is not a good thing — particularly diabetics and pre-diabetics who aren't able to keep their serum glucose levels in check. But for those who are healthy — and don't eat a lot of fat in their smoothies — their blood sugar will drop quite quickly after eating their smoothies. (Fat will slow the effectiveness of insulin in the blood stream and cause blood sugar levels to stay higher for a longer period of time.)"
>
> Personally I would also like to refer to Dr Gabriel Cousens, MD book "There is a Cure for Diabetes", where he documents how he has cured or at least helped many people with diabetes and other severe illnesses to regain full vital health. I have been drinking green juices and smoothies for a very long time and I am managing my diabetes very well; however we are all different and everybody has to check and decide for themselves.

What you will need

Equipment:
- Blendtec (or other) blender, chopping board, sharp knife, spatula
- Juicer
- A pretty glass!

Base ingredients:
- It is always good to have some more watery green veggies as a base, such as celery, lettuce, spinach and cucumber

- I always put ginger and at least ½ lemon into my green juice, I like the spiciness of the ginger and the tartness the lemon adds to it
- After that it is up to you and what nature has to offer: beet greens, broccoli (I use the large leaves as well as the stems and reserve the pretty broccoli flowers for salads), kale, parsley, chives, dill, even the green tops from the carrots – anything green.

This kind of pure green juice is very potent and it may take a little getting used to. It will very quickly detox and you may even observe some flu like symptoms such as runny nose, slight diarrhea, even itching of the skin – all signs that your body is getting rid of toxins. Use small amounts first and then slowly increase. I drink at least 1-2 quarts a day, preferably in the morning but I have been doing this for a long time.

If you want your green juice to be a little "gentler" feel free to add some more sweet fruit to it like apples, oranges, even a bit of banana; I also use the hard inner core of pineapples rather than putting it into the compost. The detox effect will not be as quick and intense as with the pure green juice but maybe a softer way to ease into your green juice adventure, besides if you are a diabetic watch for the fruit sugars.

*"Let food be thy medicine
and medicine be thy food"
~Hippocrates*

super green juice #1 (made w juicer)

R, V, Veg, D

Makes 1 large glass

A handful of kale (if using the stems, cut in small chunks)

Handful of fennel bulb stalks or celery

2 handfuls of parsley

1/2 lemon

1 inch piece of fresh ginger

Put through juicer – enjoy!

- This can also be made in the blendtec, that way you retain and benefit from all the fiber!

super green juice #2 (made w juicer)

R, V, Veg, D

Makes 1 large glass

Handful of spinach

Handful of fennel bulb stalks or celery

1 handful of cilantro

1 orange

1 inch piece of fresh ginger

Put through juicer – enjoy!

- This can also be made in the blendtec, that way you retain and benefit from all the fiber!

super green juice #3

R, V, Veg, D

Makes 1 large glass

Handful of kale/spinach/lettuce (if using the stems, cut in small chunks)

Handful of fennel bulb stalks or celery

2 handfuls of parsley

1 apple

½ lemon

1 inch piece of fresh ginger

Put through juicer – enjoy!

- This can also be made in the blendtec, that way you retain and benefit from all the fiber!

super green juice #4 made in blendtec

R, V, Veg, D

Makes 1 large glass

Just a small variation

Handful of kale (if using the stems, cut in small chunks)
Handful fresh cannabis leaves
handful of dill
1 carrot, 1 pear
1/2 lemon
1 inch piece of fresh ginger
1 cup of filtered water

1 tbl sp of chlorella or spirulina powder (optional)
blend in high power blender – enjoy! (I am experimenting with raw cannabis to lower my blood sugar and NO it does not make you high but gives you at least all the benefits of other dark leafy greens if not more)

today's super juice with everything (almost) made in blendtec

R, V, Veg, D

Makes 1 large glass

Handful of each kale (if using the stems, cut in small chunks), parsley, dill, oak leaf (or other lettuce)

A sprig of each peppermint and lemon balm

1 stalk celery

1 small orange

1/2 lemon

1 inch piece of fresh ginger

2 small peaches

1 cup of filtered water

blend in high power blender – this version is a little sweeter because of all the fruit, but ohhhhh so delicious

other smoothies and juices

ruby red beet and blueberry juice

R, V, Veg, D

Makes 1 large glass

1 large or 2 small ruby red beets

1 large handful of blueberries (frozen is fine)

½ inch fresh ginger and ½ lemon

½ cup – 1 cup filtered water (depending on how thick you like it)

Put all ingredients into blendtec and blend at high speed until smooth.

coconut/pineapple smoothie

R, V, Veg, D
Makes 1 large glass

One of my favorite smoothies is made with fresh coconut. Sometimes they are hard to find depending on where you live. Here in Colorado we are pretty far from the tropics so most of the time the coconuts are a bit too dried out and/or super expensive. But a few weeks ago in California I found the most amazing and fresh coconut I've ever had. Here is what I made from it:

I emptied out the nutritious coconut water to drink pure and of course use part of it in the smoothie. The inner soft layer of coconut meat needs to be scraped out with a large spoon. I put part of it into the blender, added fresh pineapple and some of the coconut water. No need for sweetener!!! Blend till very smooth and enjoy. Tastes like pina colada without the alcohol – and so delicious and healthy.

banana/raw cacao/almond butter smoothie

R, V, Veg, D   *Makes 1 large glass*

Put into blender:

1 ripe banana, 1 heaped tbl sp raw cacao powder, 1 heaped tbl sp Almond Butter, ½ tsp cinnamon powder, 3-4 cups almond milk, blend till smooth – enjoy!

This recipe is very sweet even without adding any sweetener, so again, be aware if you are diabetic. Harder fruit and veggies are suited very well for the juicer. Softer ones such as peaches, bananas, pears etc are better used in smoothies.

carrot/apple/ginger juice

R, V, Veg, D   *Makes 1 large glass or 2 small ones*

Put through juicer or use blendtec (then add ½ -1 cup filtered water):

2 large carrots, 1 apple, one 1-2 inch piece of ginger, ½ lemon

!Immune booster par excellence!

> (try replacing the apple with an orange, mandarin or tangerine – very good also; but again sweet, so be careful if you have to watch your blood sugar)

carrot/beet/ginger juice

R, V, Veg, D

Makes 1 large glass

Put through juicer:

2 large carrots, 1 beet root, one 1-2 inch piece of ginger, ½ lemon

(replace the beet or add to juice the inner hard core of a pineapple that you usually would toss out or compost – put it through the juicer as well, adds a tropical flavor to it)

2 breakfasts

"If you don't take care of your body, where are you going to live?" ~Unknown

blue corn and berries pancakes with toasted pine nuts

R, C, V, Veg, D

2-4 servings

1 cup almond milk

6 Tbl sp coconut oil/butter, melted

¼ tbl sp stevia

3/4 tsp Celtic sea salt salt

1 tbl sp vanilla

2 large eggs (or equivalent amount of chia/flax seeds)

1 cup blue corn flour

1 cup spelt or buckwheat flour

1 tbl sp ground cinnamon

1/2 cup fresh or frozen blueberries (or any berries that are in season)

freshly grated zest of 1/2 organic orange

½ cup toasted pine nuts

Stir to combine all of the ingredients in a large bowl.

Heat frying pan (I use a ceramic covered one) and coat lightly with coconut oil. Place either several table spoons of batter to have smaller pancakes or fill entire pan to make one big one. Cook for roughly 4-6 minutes on each side or until golden brown. Sprinkle with the toasted pine nuts and more berries. Serve immediately.

toasted sprouted grain bread with fruit and raw cacao nibs

R, C, V, Veg, D

Makes 1 serving

1 slice of toasted sprouted grain bread (Ezekiel)

½ ripe banana and a few slices of mango or other fresh fruit

½ tbl sp raw cacao nibs, sliced, toasted almonds

Mash up banana onto toast, sprinkle with cacao nibs and sliced almonds, decorate with mango or other fresh fruit.

oven baked berry pancake

C, V, Veg, D

Makes 1-2 servings

Ingredients:

4 large eggs (for vegan version replace w equal amount of soaked chia/flax seeds)

1 cup almond milk

1 cup spelt flour

½ tsp stevia

1/2 tsp freshly grated lemon or orange zest

1/4 tsp sea salt

2 tbl sp organic virgin coconut oil

1/2 cup blueberries

1/2 cup raspberries or cherries

toasted slivered almonds and a few sprigs of rosemary or peppermint for decoration

Preheat the oven to 400 degrees F.

Use a blender or hand mixer to combine the eggs, almond milk, flour, stevia, lemon zest and salt.

Warm a 12-inch skillet in oven. Add the coconut oil and melt. Pour the batter into the skillet, then scatter the berries on top. Put the pan in the oven, and bake until puffed and cooked through, about 20 minutes. Slice and serve, topped with toasted almonds (or toasted coconut flakes). Decorate with more berries if desired.

peach and cinnamon waffles

C, R, Veg, D

about 2-4 servings

1 cup lukewarm almond milk

2 tbl spn coconut oil/butter, melted

1/2 tbl spn stevia

1/4 tsp Celtic sea salt

1 tbl spn vanilla

2 large eggs (or equivalent amount of chia/flax seeds or a mashed banana)

1 cup sprouted grain or spelt flour

1 tbl sp coconut or almond flour

1 tbl spn ground cinnamon

1/2 cup peach puree

freshly grated zest of 1 large orange

1 1/2 tsp instant yeast

Stir to combine all of the ingredients in a large bowl, allowing room for expansion. Cover with plastic wrap and let sit at (warm) room temperature for an hour.

The mixture will begin to bubble somewhat.
Preheat waffle iron and coat lightly with coconut oil. Place enough batter in the center of the waffle iron to allow for expansion. Cook for roughly 4-6 minutes until golden brown. Serve immediately. Or allow to cool on a wire rack if you have left overs, then re-heat in toaster oven.

You can just sprinkle with dark chocolate and let it melt on the hot waffles, which is an easy way to have a chocolate sauce. Add some fresh fruit/berries, some more peach puree and toasted slivered almonds or pecans for decoration and added nutrition.

baked raspberry pancake

C, V, Veg, D

Makes 1-2 servings

500 ml almond milk

2 eggs (for vegan replace w equal amount of soaked chia/flax seeds)

1 cup spelt flour

1/4 cup coconut oil

1/2 tbl sp stevia

A pinch of salt

1/2 tsp vanilla essence or powder

Topping: some fresh or frozen raspberry and some stevia

Pre-heat oven to 350 degrees F.

quickly mix everything in a bowl (except the raspberries and stevia for topping) until well combined (about 1 min).

Pour the mixture into a baking dish lined with parchment paper or use stone ware. Make sure it is not too thick.

Sprinkle some raspberry and stevia on top.

Bake for about 20-30 min or until brown.

Serve with fresh fruit, toasted slivered almonds or walnuts.

apple, blackberry and vanilla cobbler

C, V, Veg, D

Makes 1-2 servings

2 cups spelt or barley flour

½ cup virgin olive oil

½ tsp stevia

⅔ cup almond or coconut milk

1 tsp lemon juice

2 tsps vanilla extract

1 apple, seeded, chopped

1 handful blackberries (fresh or frozen)

⅓ cup flaked almonds

½ tsp cinnamon

Coconut milk vanilla ice cream to serve - optional

Preheat oven to 350°F. Place the flour, oil and stevia in a food processor and process until the mixture resembles fine crumbs. Gradually add the almond milk, lemon juice and vanilla extract and process until the mixture just comes together. Place the chopped apples, blackberries in baking dish. Top with the cobbler mixture and sprinkle with the almonds and cinnamon. Bake for 35–40 minutes or until golden and cooked through. Serve with ice cream, if desired.

coconut-pineapple breakfast cake

C, V, Veg, D
Makes up to 6 servings

1 cup spelt flour
1/4 tsp cinnamon
1/2 tsp salt
1/2 tsp baking soda (the aluminum free version)
2 eggs or the equiv. amount of soaked chia or flax seed
1/2 tsp stevia
2 tsp pure vanilla extract
1 cup (240g) crushed pineapple or ripe banana
1/2 cup full-fat canned coconut or almond milk
optional ingredients: chopped macadamia nuts or walnuts, shredded coconut, rum extract

Preheat oven to 350 F. Combine all wet ingredients. In a separate bowl, combine dry and stir well. Mix dry into wet, but don't over mix. Pour into a greased or sprayed loaf pan, and cook for 35-38 minutes. Let cool at least ten minutes before going around the sides with a knife and removing from loaf pan. Spread top and/or slice with coconut butte

vegan banana muffins

C, V, Veg, D

Makes 2-4 servings

1 ripe bananas

1 tbl sp coconut oil/butter

1/2 tsp stevia

1/4 cup organic spelt flour

¼ cup organic coconut flour

¼ cup organic rolled oats

Pinch of salt

1/4 tsp baking soda

1/4 tbl sp cinnamon

1/4 tsp ground nutmeg

1/4 tsp ground ginger

¼ cup each chocolate chips and dried cherries

walnuts or pecans (optional)

Preheat oven to 360 degrees

Cream oil with stevia. In a separate bowl mash bananas with a potato masher or fork. Add bananas to coconut oil and stevia and mix well.

Add the dry ingredients to the wet, making sure to scrape the sides and mix well. Stir in nuts at the end if you plan to use them.

Spray cooking spray in a muffin tin and add dollops of batter into each slot – 3/4 of the way full. Bake for 25 minutes. Makes 6 muffins.

premama's oatmeal cake

C, Veg, D

Makes 3-4 servings

1 1/2 cups water

1 cup old fashioned oats (not quick oats)

1/2 cup coconut oil, softened (or stir directly into the warm oats to dissolve)

1 tsp stevia

2 eggs

1 1/2 cups barley or spelt flour

1 tsp baking soda

1/2 tsp salt

2 tsp cinnamon

½ cup chocolate chips

½ cup raisins

For topping

½ tsp stevia

1 cup unsweetened shredded or flaked coconut

1 cup walnuts, chopped

More cinnamon if desired

Preheat oven to 350 degrees. Bring water to a boil in a small pot. Add the oatmeal. Stir it to combine and let sit for 20 minutes. In a mixing bowl, mix coconut oil (or dissolve coconut oil in warm oatmeal), stevia and eggs until fluffy. Add oatmeal mixture and mix well. Add flour, baking soda, chocolate chips, raisins, salt and cinnamon, and mix on low just until flour is incorporated. Pour into a greased 9×13 pan. Bake for 30 minutes.

For the topping, combine all ingredients and sprinkle over top. Be careful to watch while baking as the coconut flakes brown very quickly, you can cover the pan with foil or just add the coconut flakes just before cake is done.

baked cherry french toast

C, V, Veg, D *Makes 2-3 servings*

2 ripe bananas

1 cup coconut milk

1 tbl sp vanilla

1 tsp cardamom, 1/8 tsp nutmeg, 1/8 tsp cinnamon

1 tbl sp spelt or coconut flour

1/2 tsp sea salt

1 loaf sprouted grain bread (or six slices of the frozen version)

Coconut oil (optional)

1 bag pitted frozen black cherries

Put all ingredients into the food processor, except the bread and coconut oil and process to a smooth batter. Toast the bread then rip into 3-4 inch pieces, put first layer into oiled baking pan, cover with some of the batter and part of the cherries. Repeat until all bread, batter and cherries are used up. Bake in oven at 350 degrees F for about 45 minutes to an hour. Let cool to lukewarm before eating. Warm leftovers in oven and enjoy the next

vanilla gRAWnola

R, V, Veg, D

½ cup (dry) oatmeal (I used old-fashioned oats)

1 cup almonds

½ cup toasted coconut flakes

1/4 cup coconut oil

1/4 cup chia seed

1/4 cup dried cherries

1 tsp stevia

1 tbl tsp vanilla

In food processor chop almonds and cherries, then add all other ingredients till well combined. Store in an airtight container and keep refrigerated for up to 2 weeks.

Feel free to be creative and substitute

chopped dried fruit (apricots, dates, raisins, etc.), dried berries (cranberries, blueberries etc.) chopped pecans, walnuts, or sunflower seeds

Eat with added fresh berries or other seasonal fruit and almond milk.

goji berry/raw cacao nibs/almond gRAWnola

R, V, Veg, D

Makes 6-10 servings

Chop the almonds in the food processor, add raw, organic coconut oil, stevia, raw organic vanilla powder, pulse, add Cacao Nibs and Goji Berries (or raw Hunza raisins- they are the best) and gently pulse, being careful not to crush the berries and cacao nibs. Add soaked chia seeds and a pinch of sea salt, pulse to combine. Don't over process. Play with amounts until to your liking.

Spread on silicon sheets and put into food dehydrator, dry at no more than 115 degrees F (to preserve enzymes). Check often, if half dry, carefully flip over and remove silicon sheets, finish drying process on ventilated drying rack, this can take overnight. When completely dry, scrape into large wide bowl and leave out to dry and cool for several hours. Don't worry if the pieces break, you want to break them into granola sized bits anyway.

This is a very healthy, low carb/grain free alternative to your regular granola. Add fresh fruit and serve with coconut or almond milk (unsweetened of course) and enjoy!!

Here it is fresh and moist in the dehydrator

I dried it for about 2 hours at no more than 115 degrees F (to keep the enzymes alive). Then turned the dehydrator off over night. Here in Colorado the air is so dry that I can save on energy that way. In the morning I flipped the trays over, peeled the silicon sheets off and dried for another hour just on the rack. Then I break it into pieces and let dry some more in a large open bowl.

I am using an Excalibur dehydrator with 4 drying racks. Works for me, if you have a larger crowd to feed you might want to consider a larger one.

If you live in a more moist climate you may want to completely dry it in the dehydrator AND leave it in the bowl some more to make sure it is really crunchy. After that I break it into granola sized bites and store it in jar, it does not need to be refrigerated.

This is a wonderful alternative if someone shouldn't have grains, has to watch their carb intake and to avoid sugar. If you are VERY sugar conscious you might want to leave the dried berries out as well.

It is a great, healthy, sustaining breakfast if you add some fresh fruit and almond milk to it. But I sometimes snack on it just if you would eat a granola bar. Very satisfying and good for you.

3 salads

"Health is a state of complete harmony of the body, mind and spirit. When one is free from physical disabilities and mental distractions, the gates of the soul open."
~B.K.S. Iyengar

What you will need

    Equipment:
- A mandolin, spiral slicer (optional), chopping board, sharp knife, spatula

roasted choggia beet/peaches/kale salad w toasted pine nuts

I thinned out beets today so I got the lovely baby beets that are so tender and sweet and of course the recipe evolved by itself!

R, C, V, Veg, D

Makes 1-2 servings

3-4 leaves of kale (preferably dinosaur, but any will do)

2-3 beet green leaves

2 small beet roots (I used choggia beet and the regular deep dark ruby red one)

1 small zucchini

1 small peach

Dill, cilantro, peppermint leaves

1/4 tsp Celtic sea salt

Pepper to taste

1 tbl sp extra-virgin olive oil for the dressing and

1 tbl sp of peanut oil to bake the beet root

Freshly squeezed juice of 1/2 lemon

Toasted pine nuts, Red onion

Trim the bottom few inches off the kale stems and discard or use for your green smoothie. Slice the kale and beet greens into very thin ribbons, leave some whole for decoration, quarter the zucchini, dice red onions; cut beet into small sections, put into baking dish, toss w peanut oil and bake until tender. Allow beet to cool off a bit. Add pine nuts, kale, zucchini, slice peach right into salad , add the dill, chopped peppermint and cilantro; add 1/4 tsp of salt, add 3 tbl sp oil, lemon juice, pepper, walnuts and toss.

raw tuscan kale salad

R, V, Veg, D

Makes 1-2 servings

1 bunch kale (preferably dinosaur, but any will do)

2 garlic cloves

1/4 tsp sea salt

3 tbl sp extra-virgin olive oil

Freshly squeezed juice of one lemon

1/8 tsp red pepper flakes

Walnuts, celery, Red and green onions

Trim the bottom few inches off the kale stems and save for your green juice.. Slice the kale into very thin ribbons. Place the kale in a large bowl. Using a mandolin slice celery and red onions very thin; slice the white part of the green onions, add walnuts, crush the garlic over the kale add 1/4 tsp of salt, add 3 tbl sp oil, lemon juice, pepper flakes, walnuts and toss.

This is a beautiful blend of textures and flavors, add a piece of home baked whole grain toasted bread and a glass of cabernet or shiraz… and voila… a delicious, quick meal that puts you right on a piazza in Tuscany.

black beans/red rice salad/sweet potatoes and pomegranate seeds

R, C, V, Veg, D

Makes 1-2 servings

2/3 cup black beans

2/3 cup red rice

1 sweet potato

1/2 tsp sweet smoked Spanish paprika

1/4 tsp sea salt

3 tbl sp olive oil, divided

1/2 cup pecans or cashews, coarsely chopped

1 1/2 tbl sp lemon juice

Pepper to taste

2 tbl sp sliced green onions or Italian parsley

Diced shallot

1/2 cup pomegranate seeds

Boil rice and beans (separately)

Preheat oven to 375° F. Cube sweet potato and toss with paprika, salt, and 1 tbsp. oil. Spread on a baking sheet in a single layer and roast, stirring occasionally, until browned and tender, about 30 minutes. Let cool. Spread pecans or cashews on another baking sheet and toast until fragrant, stirring once, 6 to 8 minutes.

Whisk together remaining 2 tbsp. oil, the lemon juice, more paprika, salt and pepper in a serving bowl. Toss with reserved rice, beans, roasted sweet potato, green onions/parsley, and most of pecans/cashews and pomegranate seeds. Sprinkle with remaining pecans and pomegranate seeds.

Find red rice (also called Bhutanese Rice) and smoked Spanish paprika at Whole Foods Market or other well-stocked grocery stores.

raw lasagna

Sunburst squash lasagna with tomato, cashew ricotta and tomato/rosemary sauce on a bed of arrugula

R, V, Veg, D

You will need a spiral slicer that makes those beautiful spirals and paper thin slices of veggies but you can try cutting them with a real sharp knife.

Place the arrugula on the plate, arrange sliced sunburst squash (or zucchini) on top, cover with

cashew ricotta –

Soak natural cashews for about 1-2 hours in spring water, then place in food processor w garlic, preserved lemon (or lemon juice and some rind), a little water, sea salt, process to creamy consistency.

Place thinly sliced tomatoes on top cover with

tomato/rosemary sauce –

Organic sundried tomatoes, soaked for ½ hr (keep the soaking water for your veggie smoothie), some fresh tomato, lemon juice, olive oil, sea salt, pepper, process in food processor until smooth, then add diced shallots and fresh rosemary

Cover with more squash and tomatoes, sprinkle w more rosemary

That's it, a glass of organic red goes with it beautifully; I also had some "raw" crackers with it. Enjoy!

brown quinoa/tomato salad

R, C, V, Veg, D

Makes 1-2 servings

Boil 1 cup of brown quinoa in two cup of water until soft (appr. 20 min), allow to cool a little. Meanwhile, chop 1 tomato, 1 small red onion, a few green onions or chives, a handful of flat leaf parsley, dice 1 cl of garlic. Squeeze ½ lemon, combine with 1 tbl sp olive oil, add Celtic sea salt, black ground pepper and 1 tbl sp sundried tomatoes (the ones that come in oil). Whisk all ingredients together in large salad bowl. Arrange on a bed of greens and sprinkle with toasted pine nuts or walnuts.

For salad: any mix of greens will do, see some of my other recipes.

baked roots with homemade mayonnaise and kale salad in ginger/lemon dressing

R, C, V, Veg, D

makes about 1-2 servings

baked roots

1 large sweet potato

1-2 ruby red or choggia beets

1 tbl spoon peanut or coconut oil

½ tsp Celtic sea salt

Chop potato and beets into squares, mix all ingredients and bake till done (about 40-45 min at 375 degrees F)

kale salad with ginger/lemon dressing

1 large handful of kale (I used Red Russian)

½ inch of fresh ginger root

½ tsp Celtic sea salt

A few pitted black olives

1 tbl sp lemon juice

1 tbl sp olive oil

Red pepper flakes

Shred the kale into small ribbons right into your salad bow, finely grate ginger in as well, add all other ingredients except the red pepper flakes, massage dressing into kale (I love to use my hands to do that)

Arrange on plate and top with halved olives and the red pepper flakes to make it look pretty and colorful.

homemade mayonnaise

2 tbl sp mayonnaise (use the vegan option or fat free if you like)

1 tbl sp chopped flat leaf parsley and dill

2 diced cloves of garlic

A few slices of red onion

A pinch of Celtic sea salt

Mix all ingredients and serve with the roasted roots.

shredded kale with warm brussels sprouts and toasted walnuts in a shallot, dijon mustard/ginger dressing

R, C, V, Veg, D

Makes 1-2 servings

1 tbl sp Lemon juice

1 tsp Dijon mustard

1 minced shallot

½ tsp sea salt

black pepper

1 tbl sp Walnut oil

½ tsp grated fresh ginger

Whisk all ingredients together in large salad bowl

for salad

Shredded kale

Brussels sprouts (preferably small), trimmed and halved lengthwise (quartered if large)

walnut halves

1 tsp salt

Mandolin sliced red cabbage and apples

Preheat oven to 450°F.

Toss sprouts in pan with walnut oil, and salt. Arrange sprouts, cut sides down, in 1 layer, nuts at the side and roast in lower third of oven until undersides of sprouts are golden and nuts are fragrant, 12 to 15 minutes.

Whisk vinaigrette, then transfer warm sprouts and nuts to a large bowl and toss with other ingredients.

ezekiel sprouted grain veggie wraps

R, V, Veg, D

Makes 1-2 servings

On Ezekiel Sprouted Grain Wrap:

Spread a mashed avocado seasoned with lemon juice, Celtic sea salt, pepper and garlic on the Ezekiel Sprouted Grain Wrap. On top put shredded kale, parsley, chives and dill along with a sliced red onion and if you like some tender young broccoli (it just happened to be perfectly ripe in the greenhouse) or tomato/cucumber, zucchini, green beans, artichoke, black beans (no limits to your creativity here), roll up, if necessary secure with a tooth pick, arrange on a bed of lettuce or eat by itself. If you add the lettuce here is a delicious dressing:

Put into blender: roasted, peeled red pepper, lemon juice, garlic, red onion, some balsamic vinaigrette, olive oil, Celtic sea salt and pepper; add filtered water until you have the desired thickness.

So much better than the store bought readymade dressings and you know what's in it!!!

And here is a picture with more detail

cucumber/kelp noodle salad

R, V, Veg, D

Makes 1-2 servings

Slice 1 English Cucumber, a small red onion and a small Jalapeno pepper with a mandolin, add a handful of kelp noodles, add ½ tsp grated fresh ginger and 1 handful of shredded cilantro, season with Celtic sea salt, 1 tbl sp lemon juice, olive oil and some red pepper flakes.

green/verte/gruen...
can't get any greener than this salad

R, V, Veg, D

Makes 1-2 servings

I picked what was ready to harvest today:

Oak leaf lettuce, Russian Kale, tender fresh dill, Black Seeded Curly Green Lettuce and spinach for the green salad, sprinkled it with Celtic sea salt, a few drops of lemon juice and a dash of extra virgin olive oil.

For some more substance I added a green lentil salad with grape tomatoes, more shredded Russian kale, chives, diced jalapeno pepper, diced red onions, Celtic sea salt, lemon juice and sesame oil. I think it would also be lovely with some fresh cilantro.

As a little extra bonus I toasted some Indian Pappadam to go along with it and a gentle Chardonnay!

R, V, Veg, D
Makes 1-2 servings

And here is another one: oak leaf, a variety of kale (Tuscan, Red Russian, Dinosaur), dill, parsley, lemon balm, peppermint, chives, basil, head lettuce; with just a drizzle of balsamic vinegar and extra virgin olive oil.

4 cooked and raw dishes

"The doctor of the future will no longer treat the human frame with drugs, but rather will cure and prevent disease with nutrition."
~Thomas Edison

☙

What you will need

Equipment:
- A mandolin, spiral slicer (optional), chopping board, sharp knife, spatula

layered sweet potato/black bean/ guacamole tortilla

R, C, V, Veg, D

Makes 1-2 servings

sweet potato mix

1 cup roasted sweet potatoes (cooled off)

A pinch of each: cumin, red pepper flakes, Celtic sea salt

1 tbl sp coconut milk

1 tbl sp lemon juice

1 tsp chipotle paste

1 diced garlic glove

for the black bean mix

1 cup cooked black beans (cooled off)

½ cup brown quinoa (cooled off)

Put all ingredients into food processor, blend until smooth with still a few chunky pieces. Set aside.

guacamole

1 ripe avocado mashed

Add a tbl sp diced red onions, 1 tbl sp chopped cilantro, a pinch of each: Celtic sea salt, red pepper flakes

1 tbl sp lemon juice

assembly

With kitchen scissors cut 1 Ezekiel Sprouted Grain Tortilla in quarters, toast till crisp, allow to cool, then spread sweet potato mix on first layer, sprinkle with black beans and quinoa, top with another quarter piece of tortilla, spread with the guacamole mix and top with black beans and quinoa, cover with third layer and use up the sweet potato mix, if you have enough, add a fourth layer of tortilla with another guacamole spread.

I happened to have a perfectly ripe baby corn ready to harvest from the greenhouse so I added it to my display. Feel free to do the same.

zucchini and purple potato fritters with jalapeno vegannaise

C, Veg, D

Makes 2 servings

In a mixing bowl beat 2 eggs with ½ cup almond milk, ½ tsp Celtic sea salt, a pinch of nutmeg. Add 2 tbl sp spelt flower, 2 minced garlic cloves and mix well, pour half of the mixture in another bowl.

Grate the zucchini, then the purple potato, keep them separate.

Slice a medium sized yellow onion.

Put zucchini in bowl with the egg mixture, add half of the onion and ½ tsp dried basil. Combine.

Put purple potato in the other bowl with egg mixture, add ½ tsp fennel seed and the other half of the onions. Combine well.

In a ceramic coated pan heat 1-2 tbl sp peanut oil and set small batches of the zucchini mixture (I used a little less than the size of the palm of my hand), fry golden on each side, set on wire rack and continue with all of the mixture, then do the same with the purple potato mix.

In the meantime chop about 1 inch of a jalapeno pepper, mix into 2 tbl sp vegannaise (vegan mayonnaise), add 1 tbl sp chopped chives, a few drops of lemon juice and some Celtic sea salt. Mix well.

Serve along with the fritters and a mixed green salad.

coconut french green lentils and beans curry

C, V, Veg, D

Makes 1-2 servings

1-2 tbl sp coconut oil

one medium sized yellow onion (chopped)

2 garlic cloves (diced)

1 red pepper (chopped or diced)

½ cup pre-cooked green French lentils

1 cup pre-cooked French baby green beans

2 large handfuls of spinach

1-2 cups coconut milk

1 tb sp lime or lemon juice

1-2 tea sp turmeric.

Celtic sea salt

dried powdered jalapeno pepper and ginger

red pepper flakes

In a ceramic covered pan warm some coconut oil, sauté one medium sized yellow onion (chopped), 2 garlic cloves (diced), 1 red pepper (chopped or diced). Cook for 5-8 minutes on medium heat. Add ½ cup pre-cooked green French lentils, 1 cup pre-cooked French baby green beans, 2 large handfuls of spinach, 1-2 cups coconut milk, 1 tb sp lime or lemon juice, 1-2 tea sp turmeric. Simmer for about 10 minutes, season with Celtic sea salt, dried powdered jalapeno pepper and ginger; sprinkle with red pepper flakes. Serve over brown or red rice or eat with pappadam.

This is also lovely when you add some pre-cooked or baked chopped sweet potatoes.

the ultimate veggie wrap

Today's harvest and lunch ingredients:

R, V, Veg, D
Makes 1 serving

veggie wrap

We will need (feel free to substitute, I just use what is ripe in the garden)

a large cabbage leaf (I used red cabbage because I like the color) for the wrap; place flat on your chopping board, carefully slice off some of the harder part of the stem and reserve for your smoothie.

julienned rainbow carrots, beets, baby green beans and baby red onions, tender broccoli flowers, chopped greens tops from the onions, chives, dill, Celtic sea salt, fresh ground pepper, seaweed strips (I used nori sheets and snipped them right onto the veggies)

nut and seed raw vegan non-dairy cheese

A small handful of walnuts,

1 tbl sp soaked chia or flax seeds

½ tbl sp nutritional yeast flakes

1 tbl sp lemon juice

Dill, 1 clove garlic

Celtic sea salt, pepper

Put all in food processor, pulse till resembles consistency of cream cheese. Spread cheese on red cabbage leaf, arrange all veggies on top (don't overfill), fold bottom part of leaf over 1/3 or veggies, roll up from side just like you would with a regular wrap. Allow some of the veggies to show at the top.

avocado nori rolls

R, V, Veg, D

Makes 1-2 servings

nori rolls

Mash ripe avocado with a sprinkle of lemon juice and Celtic sea salt, add finely chopped dill and diced garlic, mix well. Place a spoon full on Nori sheets (I used the small ones (appr. 2.5x4 inches) but the larger ones work as well) and roll up. Place on plate.

Salad: I used oak leaf as I have plenty in the garden and is my favorite, but any will do. Roughly chop, add diced red onion, chives, sun dried tomatoes, toss with lemon juice and a little olive oil. Sprinkle cashews on top. Garnish with tiny broccoli rosettes and baby green beans.

nori rolls and red lentil salad

R, C, V, Veg, D

Makes 1-2 servings

nori rolls

Place two nori sheets so they overlap on the longer side, mash a ripe avocado on top, season w sea salt/pepper/cumin, place some very tender bok choy leaves on top, then thinly sliced red onion, some cucumber, cilantro; roll it all up and slice diagonal.

red lentil salad

Cook red lentils

Make sauce: organic French mustard, freshly grated ginger root, lemon juice, sesame oil, garlic, sea salt, pepper/ turmeric/cumin, water to thin

Mix red lentils with sauce, cucumber cubes, cilantro, red onions

arrange everything nicely on plates with tender bok choy leaves for decoration.

chipotle-kissed red bean, red pepper and sweet potato chili

R, C, V, Veg, D

Makes 2-4 servings

1 tbl sp olive oil

1 medium-size yellow onion, chopped

1 medium-size red bell pepper, seeded and chopped (or dried Red Pepper)

1 large garlic clove, minced

1 tb sp chili powder, or more to taste

1 tb sp Indian Spice mix – fennel, fenugreek, mustard seeds, cumin

1 1/2 lbs sweet potatoes, peeled and cut into 1/2 inch chunks

one 14.5 oz can crushed tomatoes

One 15.5 oz can dark red kidney beans

1 1/2 cups water

Salt

1 tbl sp minced canned chipotle chilies in adobo sauce, or to taste

Heat the oil over medium heat. Add the onion, bell pepper, and garlic, cover, and cook until softened, about 5 minutes. Stir in the chili powder and Indian Spice and cook for 30 seconds. Add the sweet potatoes and stir to coat with the spices.

Cook for 10 min then add the tomatoes, beans and water; season with salt, cover, and cook on 45 min.. When ready to serve, stir the chipotles in the chili.

sweet potato burger

R, C, V, Veg, D

Makes 1-2 servings

1 can cannellini white beans, drained or dark red kidney beans

1 large sweet potato, baked/peeled/mashed (about 2 cups)

2 tbl sp tahini

1 tsp lemon pepper

1/4 cup spelt flour

salt to taste if needed

sunflower oil for pan

burgers: avocado, Dijon mustard, sprouted grain toast, spinach/arugula leaves, sunflower sprouts, red onion, olive oil, pepper (or use guacamole)

Bake or boil sweet potato, place in large mixing bowl.
Add drained beans to mixing bowl. Mash beans and potato together.

Mash in seasoning and flour. The mixture will be soft and moist. Add more flour to be able to form a patty if necessary.

Heat 1 tbl sp safflower oil in a pan over high heat.

Form a patty from mixture, drop patty in the pan. Repeat until the pan is filled. Cook until browned on both sides. You could also bake.

Transfer cooked patties to paper towel. Cool for a few minutes.

Serve on toast with your choice of toppings.

>It is delicious with homemade coleslaw.

alfalfa sprouts/avocado/nori sandwich with salad

R, C, V, Veg, D

Makes 1-2 servings

toast a slice of Ezekiel sprouted grain bread, mash 1/2 avocado right on the toasted bread, cover with alfalfa sprouts, lightly salt with sea salt, snip a nori sheet on top, sprinkle with fresh ground black pepper.

Salad:

    1 tbl sp tamari soy sauce

    1 tbl sp cup lemon juice

    1/4 cup extra virgin olive oil

¼ tsp sea salt

1/2 medium size red onion

Handful of cashews

Handful of pumpkin seeds

1/2 pound fresh kale (de-stemmed and cut into ¼ inch ribbons)

1 handful of Italian Parsley, chopped

1/4 cup sunflower seed sprouts

1/4 cup alfalfa sprouts

1/2 avocado cut into 1/2 inch cubes (optional)

1/2 cup thinly sliced yellow bell peppers (optional)

½ cup shredded red cabbage

Combine dressing ingredients, slice the onion into half moons and marinate in the dressing as you prepare the rest of the salad.

Toss all ingredients with the dressing, let sit for a few minutes for flavors to develop.

green lentil and asparagus soup

C, V, Veg, D

Makes 1-2 servings

soak the green lentils over night (2 cups), rinse well and boil in fresh water until tender. Drain and reserve. Boil asparagus (3-4 spears), reserve the tips, cut stems in small chunks, liquefy chunks and cooking water in blender, pass through sieve. Sauté 1 onion and 1 garlic clove until translucent, add1 large sliced portabella mushroom and cook until tender. Add green lentils, asparagus tip and broth, finely shred some dinosaur or other kale, add to soup and let simmer a few minutes. Add Celtic sea salt, a bit of fennel powder and pepper to taste.

broccoli/avocado/quinoa warm salad

R, C, V, Veg, D   *Makes 1-2 servings*

I got inspired by this recipe as a friend had posted it for me. I adjusted it a little: Steam or boil the broccoli till it still has a bite, (I am using the stems to puree and make it into a cream of broccoli with coconut milk tomorrow. I cut the other half into little florets. Tossed with some quinoa, sliced avocado, Italian parsley and a drizzle of chili pepper oil; I added twice baked sweet potato which enhanced and balanced the flavors even more. Baked it in aluminum foil first, then cut in half, mashed a little, drizzled with the chili infused oil and seasoned with sea salt.

mushroom and sundried tomato quiche

R, Veg (ovo), D   Makes 3-4 servings

ingredients:

mushroom mix:

1 tbl sp of peanut oil

1 chopped onion or shallot

2 diced cloves of garlic

2 handfuls of sliced or chopped Portobello mushrooms

2 handfuls of shredded kale

1 tbl sp of sundried julienned

crust:

2 eggs (or equivalent amount of soaked chia or flaxseeds)

2 tbl sp of coconut oil

1 tsp Celtic sea salt

a pinch of nutmeg

1 cup of spelt flour or sprouted grain flour

½ tsp baking powder

egg mixture

2 eggs

½ cup almond milk

½ tsp Celtic sea salt

fresh ground black pepper, diced garlic, a pinch of nutmeg

finish and garnish

quartered artichokes (from a jar in water)

more julienned sundried tomatoes

fresh thyme, fresh rosemary.

Heat a 1 tbl sp of peanut oil; sauté 1 chopped onion or shallot, 2 diced cloves of garlic; add 2 handfuls of sliced or chopped Portobello mushrooms until nice and brown, add 2 handfuls of shredded kale and 1 tbl sp of sundried julienned tomatoes. Allow to cool.

in the meantime prepare crust:

In a food processor mix 2 eggs (or equivalent amount of soaked chia or flaxseeds), 2 tbl sp of coconut oil, 1 tsp Celtic sea salt, a pinch of nutmeg. Add spelt flour or sprouted grain flour and ½ tsp baking powder, process until a ball forms, if needed add a little water or more flour.

Use an 8 inch stoneware baking dish, rub with coconut oil, with your hand put into a fist press dough into mold, raising it at the edges about 1.5 inches. Make sure thickness is even, level out the raised edges, pierce center several times with a fork.

batter:

Use same mixing bowl, add 2 eggs, ½ cup almond milk, ½ tsp Celtic sea salt, fresh ground black pepper, diced garlic, a pinch of nutmeg, process until well blended.

Spread mushroom mixture evenly over dough, pour egg batter on top. Decorate with quartered artichokes, more julienned sundried tomatoes, fresh thyme, fresh rosemary.

Bake in pre heated oven for about 45min to 1hr at 350 degrees F. Let cool till lukewarm and serve with a fresh green salad.

5 appetizers

"To insure good health: eat lightly, breathe deeply, live moderately, cultivate cheerfulness, and maintain an interest in life."
~William Londen

savory blue corn waffles with guacamole

C, V, Veg, D

Makes about 6-8 small waffles

Ingredients

1 cup blue cornmeal

1 tbl sp chia seeds

1 tbl sp roasted yellow corn

1 tbl sp coconut oil (melted)

1 tsp baking powder

1 tsp salt

1 cups low-fat almond milk

1 tbl sp lemon juice

1 large egg (or equivalent amount of soaked chia or flaxseeds)

1 tsp baking yeast

In a large bowl, combine all wet ingredients first, then add dry ingredients

Preheat waffle iron, coat w some coconut oil

Pour about 1 cup of batter into the waffle iron and cook through until nicely crisp and browned.

guacamole

Mash 1 ripe avocado with 1 tsp lemon or lime juice, small handful of chopped cilantro, ½ tsp Celtic sea salt, 1 tsp diced red onion, 1 tsp diced jalapeno pepper (add some roasted yellow corn if you like)

Arrange all on plate and sprinkle with toasted pine nuts to give it an even more Southwestern flavor. The roasted yellow corn adds some lovely sweetness and crunch to the dish.

vegan cheeses

(rosemary/basil/garlic)

R, V, Veg, D

Makes 2-4 servings

2 cups of raw cashews (or almonds, peeled) soaked in water over night, drain the next day, put in blender or food processor with 1 tbl sp lemon juice, 1 tbl sp nutritional yeast, 1 tsp pro-biotic powder, 1 tsp. sea salt, pulse till very fine and has sticky consistency (if it's too dry add some filtered water), scrape into bowl, portion off a good handful (that way you get 3 individual little cheeses) and mold into little patties, gently roll one into finely chopped rosemary, the other into dried basil and the last one in a mixture of diced garlic and coarse sea salt, if you like you can drizzle them with organic virgin olive oil (prep time without soaking about 20 minutes!!) You can leave them on the kitchen counter for a day to cure, then store in the fridge up to a week. They never last this long for me they are just too good.. ...

walnut/rosemary pate on sprouted grain toast

R, C, V, Veg, D

Makes 2-4 servings

While you are toasting your sprouted grain bread prepare the pate.

In a food processor combine a handful of walnuts, 1 tsp nutritional yeast, 2 tbl sp lemon juice, ½ tsp Celtic sea salt, 1 tbl sp fresh rosemary leaves, fresh ground black pepper, 1 clove garlic. Process until it has the consistency of a pate. Spread on sprouted grain bread and serve with a mixed green salad

red and yellow grape tomatoes and basil appetizer

R, V, Veg, D

Makes 1 serving

Just a few perfectly (preferable just picked) grape tomatoes, fresh basil leaves (some chopped, some kept whole for decoration), diced garlic, a drizzle of Balsamic vinegar and olive oil, Celtic sea salt and fresh ground pepper. Add a few olives if you like. You won't miss the mozzarella, I promise!!!

artichoke spread with garlic and lemon

R, C, V, Veg, D

Makes 1-2 servings

10 oz jar artichoke hearts in olive oil, drained (or the one in water)

1 clove garlic

Juice of ½ lemon

3 tbl sp chopped fresh parsley; and/or fresh rosemary

a dash of extra virgin olive oil, Celtic sea salt

Pinch of freshly cracked black pepper

Place all ingredients in a food processor and puree until smooth. Let sit at room temperature for a few hours to allow flavors to develop. Serve with Ciabatta bread, or crudites.

lavender and sea salt toasted almonds

C, V, Veg, D

Use a salt grinder, fill with coarse grey Celtic Sea Salt and Lavender Blossoms, mix well. Put almonds into pan, grind the lavender salt onto the almonds, put a few tsps of organic coconut oil on top; put into toaster oven or regular oven, after a few minutes stir to incorporate the melted oil and salts with the almonds. Toast for about 10-15 minutes at 350 degrees or until fragrant and lightly browned (watch carefully to not burn the almonds). Add some more lavender sea salt if needed. Your kitchen will be filled with the heavenly scent of toasted almonds and lavender. Enjoy with a glass of chardonnay or shiraz!!!

6 cookies and desserts

"By cleansing your body on a regular basis and eliminating as many toxins as possible from your environment, your body can begin to heal itself, prevent disease, and become stronger and more resilient than you ever dreamed possible!"
~Dr. Edward Group III

frozen vegan almond butter/chocolate/coconut dessert

R, V, Veg, D

servings: makes one large 8 inch cake or 12 baking cups

chocolate fudge layer ingredients

3 ripe avocados

1/4 tsp salt

2 tbl sp unsweetened coconut milk

1 tsp Vanilla extract

1 tsp stevia

1/2 cup raw cacao powder

almond butter ice cream layer ingredients

1/2 cup almond butter

1/2 cup light unsweetened coconut milk

1 tsp vanilla extract

1 ripe banana

1/2 cup unsweetened shredded coconut

½ tsp stevia

ganache layer ingredients:

1 cup virgin coconut oil

1/2 cup raw cacoa powder

½ cup raw cacao nibs

½ tsp stevia

Individually blend each layer in food processor until completely smooth and place in separate bowls (to be ready for layering). Use baking cups or coat muffin tin or spring form pan with coconut oil; ganache layer comes first next the almond butter ice cream; then the chocolate fudge. Sprinkle with toasted almonds. Place in the freezer for 1-3 hours. Remove from freezer and serve immediately. To store place in a sealed tight container in the freezer.

chocolate/fruit and almond bars

R, C, V, Veg, D

Makes 6-8 servings

melt a bar of good dark bitter Chocolate (such as Lindt 90%, or Valrhona), add a tbl sp organic virgin coconut oil. Line a baking pan with parchment paper, pour chocolate and let cool for a few seconds. In the meantime toast a handful of sliced almonds and Oatmeal; in another bowl melt another tbl sp organic virgin coconut oil, when almonds and oatmeal are toasted and fragrant add to coconut oil, add small handful of raw cacao nibs, 1/2 tsp stevia, 1/2 handful of unsweetened shredded coconut, 1/4 tsp sea salt, small handful of dried cherries (or other dried fruit), toss everything with the coconut oil, spread on top of chocolate in pan, gently press into mold. Put in freezer for 10 minutes, then cut into squares and keep refrigerated afterwards. Delicious and easy to make!!

chocolate/almond bars

R, C, V, Veg, D   *Makes 6-8 servings*

a handful of each, shredded unsweetened coconut, raw cacao nibs, slivered or sliced toasted almonds. Gently melt 1-2 tbl sp organic raw coconut butter/oil, ad 1/2 tsp stevia, 1 tsp vanilla extract and the other dry ingredients. Carefully fold everything under, spread on parchment paper on a baking sheet and set in freezer for 15 minutes. Cut with sharp knife into squares. I keep mine in the freezer, they are nice and crunchy that way. Coconut oil melts easily, so they need to be stored rather cool. Usually they don't last very long, they are so delicious and healthy for you. If you are not a diabetic you could also add dried fruit such as goji berries, dried cherries etc. For those who can't tolerate coconut oil, you could probably use melted butter as well.

banana/oatmeal/cacao nibs cookies

C, V, Veg, D

Makes 6-8 servings

" NO sugar, butter, eggs or anything that can be considered unhealthy COOKIES" ; they are surprisingly light, incredibly filling and tasty. You can freeze them individually and you have an easy breakfast on the go, that contains your protein and carbs to set you up for the day.

1 1/2 cups regular rolled oats

1 cup coconut flakes

1/2 cup raw cacao nibs

1/2 tsp salt

1 tsp cinnamon

1/2 tsp allspice

1/4 cup of almond meal

1/2 cup mixed nuts, finely chopped

1 cup dried fruit (I used 1/2 chopped dried dates, and 1/2 raisins)

3 ripe bananas, mashed

1/4 cup almond or coconut oil

1 tsp vanilla extract

Preheat oven to 175C. Line baking sheet with parchment paper or use baking stone.

OR: put in dehydrator overnight

In a large bowl, combine rolled oats, almond meal, mixed nuts and coconut flakes. Stir in allspice and cinnamon. Add chopped dried fruit and stir until well and evenly mixed. In another bowl, combine oil, mashed banana and vanilla extract. Mix wet ingredients with dry ingredients and stir until well combined.

Set small mounds on baking sheet, bake for about 20 minutes or until edges are golden brown.

Or place on rack in dehydrator overnight.

raw cookies: almond/vanilla and chocolate/cardamom

R, V, Veg, D

Makes 6-8 servings

put in food processor

for each batch 3 cups of almonds, 1/2 tsp stevia, 1/2 tsp almond extract, 2 tbl sp coconut oil/butter, 1 tbl sp hemp protein powder, process till very fine and sticks together

Almond/Vanilla - add another 1 tbl sp vanilla,(if "dough" does not hold together add a little filtered water)

Chocolate/Cardamom - add 1 tsp each cinnamon, cardamom and allspice, 3 tbl sp raw cacao powder (if "dough" does not hold together add a little filtered water)

finish for both: form into roll, cut off slices, place on dehydrator sheets and dehydrate at no more than 115 degrees Fahrenheit to preserve enzymes and minerals/vitamins, leave for several hours or overnight until crunchy on outside and soft and chewy on inside. You can dust the Chocolate Cookies lightly with the raw cacao powder or press raw cacao nibs into surface before they become completely dry. Enjoy!

coconut-milk chocolate mousse with pomegranate

R, V, Veg, D
Makes 2-4 servings

beat with electric mixer 1 can of organic coconut milk, 3 tbl sp of raw cacao powder, 1/2 tsp. cinnamon, 1 tsp stevia until light and fluffy, spoon into serving dish, sprinkle with Pomegranate seeds and raw cacao nibs. (takes no more than 5 minutes to make)

gotta have them now cookies

C, Veg (ovo), D

Makes 6-8 servings

pre heat oven to 350 degrees F

2 egg whites, beat till they are shiny and stiff

add 1/2 tsp of stevia or 1-2 tbl sp of brown sugar, keep beating till dissolved; add 1 tsp vanilla, stir carefully fold under the egg whites: 2 cups of walnuts (or chopped almonds), 1/2 cup dried cherries (or cranberries), 1/2 cup raw cacao nibs (or chocolate chips), 1 cup unsweetened coconut flakes; spread on hot stone baking sheet (or regular with baking paper), bake for about 20 minutes, let cool, break into sections. Enjoy!

dark chocolate cake with coconut vanilla frosting

No flour chocolate cake suited for diabetics (with stevia)
(the version in the picture has a chocolate frosting instead and is sprinkled with raw cacao nibs and decorated with walnut halves - equally yummy!!!)

C, Veg (ovo/lacto), D   *Makes 6-8 servings*

200 g bitter chocolate (use only the best such as Valrhona, Lindt, Chocolove; otherwise your cake will be grainy)

2 sticks butter or equivalent amount of coconut oil

2 cups (or less) finely ground almonds

1 tsp stevia

4 eggs (separated)

Heat oven to 375-400 degrees F

Put baking parchment paper on bottom of spring form.

Separate eggs, beat egg whites until stiff and glistening.

Beat egg yolks with stevia until the yellow becomes much lighter

In the meantime melt chocolate and butter in double boiler.
When melted add slowly to egg yolk mixture, add almonds, finally add 1/3 of the egg whites, carefully fold under, then add the rest. Pour into spring form, bake for about 40 minutes.

coconut frosting

2 sticks (1 cup) butter or coconut oil

1 tbl sp stevia

1/4 cup cream of coconut (or, alternatively, full-fat unsweetened coconut milk)

1 tsp vanilla extract

1/2 cups flaked coconut

In a large bowl using an electric hand-mixer, cream the butter until smooth and "fluffy". Gradually add the stevia, blending until combined. Add the cream of coconut (or coconut milk), vanilla extract and coconut flakes and blend until creamy.
You can cut the cake in half and use the frosting as a filling or gently spread on top, garnishing with additional (unsweetened) coconut flakes.

peach pie

C, V, Veg, D

Makes 4-6 servings

Flourless!

2 cups almonds

1 cup oatmeal

Grind in food processor very fine

Add 1 tsp finely grated orange zest

½ tsp stevia

½ tsp baking powder

½ tsp cinnamon or pumpkin pie spice mix

Mix together

Add 1-2 tbl sp coconut oil

1 egg or substitute w equal amount of soaked chia seeds or soaked and ground flaxseeds.

Mix well with dry ingredients; if necessary and too dry add more coconut oil; if too wet add some spelt flour or more ground almonds/oatmeal

Spread into pie dish.

Cover bottom with unsweetened coconut flakes, fill up with sliced peaches.

Bake at 350 degrees F for about 45-50 minutes.

For the last 5 minutes sprinkle a mix of coconut flakes, sliced almonds and some cinnamon or spicemix, bake till almonds and coconut flakes appear toasted (be careful not to burn them).

peach pie – the raw version

R, V, Veg, D   *Makes 1-2 servings*

1/2 cup almonds

½ cup coconut flakes (unsweetened)

Grind in food processor - coarse

Add ½ tsp finely grated orange zest

½ tsp stevia

¼ tsp cinnamon

1 tsp vanilla

Add 1-2 tbl sp coconut oil

Mix until everything is well incorporated, add more coconut oil or ground almonds depending on how wet or dry it is.

Press into small baking dish (ceramic or glass), put into freezer until firm, top with sliced peaches or apricots, sprinkle w cinnamon or toasted almonds and coconut (or with raw cacao nibs). When you slice it will most likely break; it is best to make it in small dishes so it is 1 portion per person

7 salsas

The doctor of the future will give no medication; but will interest his patients in the care of the human frame, diet and in the cause and prevention of disease.
- Thomas A Edison

The sweetness of the roasted corn and the mango blends beautifully with the spiciness of the jalapeno and the cooling cilantro. For the salt – there is just nothing better out there than grey Celtic sea salt.

mango/black bean/roasted corn salsa

R, C, V, Veg, D

Makes 1-2 servings

½ perfectly ripe mango, diced

2 ears of corn, roasted on the grill, cut off the cob

1 ½ cups of cooked black beans

1 handful of cilantro, chopped

Diced red onion

Diced or crushed garlic

½ tsp coarse Celtic sea salt

1 tsp fresh diced jalapeno pepper

½ tsp fresh grated ginger

Juice of ½ lemon

1 tbl sp extra virgin olive oil

Gently toss all ingredients together, add salt and more jalapeno pepper if needed. Serve on bed of lettuce and with organic blue corn chips.

peach/tomato/roasted corn salsa

R, C, V, Veg, D

Makes 1-2 servings

1 perfectly ripe peach, diced

2 ears of corn, roasted on the grill, cut off the cob

1 chopped tomato

1 handful of cilantro, chopped

Diced red onion

Diced garlic

½ tsp coarse Celtic sea salt

1 tsp fresh diced jalapeno pepper

Juice of ½ lemon

1 tbl sp extra virgin olive oil

Gently toss all ingredients together, add salt and more jalapeno pepper if needed. Serve on bed of lettuce and with blue corn chips.

green lentil/black bean/tomato salsa

R, C, V, Veg, D

Makes 2-3 servings

1 cup cooked green lentils

1 cup cooked black beans

1 chopped tomato

1 handful cilantro, chopped

1 stalk celery finely diced

Sliced chives, Diced red onion, Diced garlic

½ tsp coarse Celtic sea salt, A pinch of cumin

1 tsp fresh diced jalapeno pepper

A pinch of red pepper flakes

Juice of ½ lemon

1 tbl sp extra virgin olive oil

Gently toss all ingredients together, add salt and more jalapeno pepper if needed. Serve on bed of lettuce and with blue corn chips.

grilled corn/black bean/peach salsa

R, C, V, Veg, D   *Makes 2-3 servings*

1 cup each grilled corn and cooked black beans

1 large or 2 small diced peaches (or substitute with cubed avocado)

1 handful of cilantro, chopped

Diced red onion

Diced garlic

½ tsp coarse Celtic sea salt

A pinch of cumin

1 tsp fresh diced jalapeno pepper

Juice of ½ lemon or lime

1 tbl sp extra virgin olive oil

Gently toss all ingredients together, add salt and more jalapeno pepper if needed. Serve on bed of lettuce and with organic blue corn chips.

8 beverages

Each cup of tea represents an imaginary voyage.
~Catherine Douzel

On a really hot summer day there is nothing more refreshing than a cold drink. Sometimes I get tired of drinking just plain water or plain iced tea all day long. Here are some delicious alternatives:

How about Green Iced Tea? I also love Iced Green Jasmin Tea. To make it even better I freeze some of the tea into ice cubes as to not water down the concoction too much.

"Where Rosemary flourished, the woman ruled."- **Unknown**

Ever had iced rosemary tea? With this one too I freeze some of the tea into ice cubes and if you like you can even add a few sprigs of rosemary into the tea or ice cubes. Makes for a beautiful display. Replace the rosemary with peppermint, lemon balm, lavender or whatever strikes your fancy for variety.

iced ginger tea; add rosemary ice cubes and/or a sprig of rosemary or peppermint!

R, C, V, Veg, D

Ginger helps the body to sweat, so toxins are drawn to the skin's surface. To prepare the ginger bath, place half-inch slices of fresh ginger in boiling water over a stove; turn off the heat, and steep for thirty minutes. Remove the ginger, and add that water into a tub already filled with hot water.

- Brenda Watson and Leonard Smith, The Detox Strategy: Vibrant Health in 5 Easy Steps

white wine spritzer

Take a pretty wine glass, add some ice cubes/crushed ice, a slice of frozen peach, ice cold filtered water and a dash of white wine. Adds a kick ..

fruit water
Use cold filtered water and frozen fruit such as blue/raspberries, peaches or whatever you like. Or freeze the fruit pieces into ice cubes and add to your water! Lovely hint of fruit and very refreshing.

9 fermented food

"... when General Lee took possession of Chambersburg on his way to Gettysburg, we happened to be a member of the Committee representing the town. Among the first things he demanded for his army was twenty-five barrels of Saur-Kraut."
Editor, The Guardian (1869)

☙

Fermented food is in many ways a wonderful union of cooked and raw. Enzymes, vitamins and life energy are amplified. Fermenting food has a long history as it is revitalizing and infusing us with living and breathing energy.

There is a wealth of scientific information about the value of fermented food and its benefits for our wellbeing available. Fermented foods are kimchi, sauerkraut, apple cider vinegar, and many more; but also wine, coffee, chocolate and beer, not quite as healthy though.

Returning to fermented foods is just a natural development if someone is on their path to healthy living, sooner or later one will experiment with them and along the process discovers its benefits and delicious taste.

Fermented food is one of the key ingredients in attaining and maintaining optimal health.

Fermentation is common, natural and present in every traditional culture around the world. In Russia, it's kefir. In China it's the thousand-year egg, a nearly black, preserved egg. For Koreans it's kimchi, a pungent side dish of fermented cabbage, garlic, and peppers. It is very well-studied for its medicinal, antimicrobial, and anti-aging qualities. For example, scientists found that chickens infected with avian flu started to recover after being fed a kimchi extract. Colombians drink a fermented corn beverage called chicha. Germans like their sauerkraut – fermented cabbage. A staple food for Hawaiians is poi, a fermented taro porridge. The Japanese add the sticky fermented soybeans called natto on top of rice. Kombucha, a fermented sweet black tea, has been adopted by cultures all over the world.

Benefits of Fermentation

Fermented foods should always be a part of our diet. The benefits of bacteria and yeasts are so important to our health and well-being that we cannot be well without them. We are designed to work in synergy with microbes.

- Fermentation neutralizes plant toxins, making vegetables more digestible.

- Fermentation of foods releases trapped vitamins and minerals from plant fibers.

- Bacteria and yeasts themselves are replete with B vitamins.

- Bacteria in the gut helps to stimulate peristalsis (fecal elimination), staving off constipation.

- Friendly bacteria keeps pathogens from gaining territory in our gut, i.e. they help keep us from getting sick.

- A mother's healthy microbial colony can prevent neonatal infections.

This is, of course, is just a brief overview when it comes to illustrating the remarkable properties of fermented food. For more detailed information and directions on fermenting and preserving I highly recommend "Preserving Food without Freezing or Canning" and "Wild Fermentation" (by Sandor Ellix Katz)

fermented cabbage

It is VERY important that all utensils are super clean. I scald the jars, lids and rubber seals (if used) right before filling the jars.

I experimented with green and red cabbage as well as "my" version of Kimchi.

for the cabbage version:

Grate the cabbage, pack firmly into the glass jar, you can add bay leaves, juniper berries, caraway/dill/celery seeds. When the jar is full pack it down with your very clean hands (fists if the opening is large enough) some more, sprinkle 1 tbl sp of Celtic sea salt (for a 1 quart container) on top, then pour boiling (filtered and non chlorinated) water over it until the cabbage is just covered. I usually wipe off any juices or leaves from the rim to keep it nice and clean. Close each jar with the lid or rubber seal and let sit on your kitchen counter for three days. Then store in your (cool) pantry, cellar or refrigerator.

Some suggest to leave the lid off and cover loosely with cheese cloth to help fermentation.

I allowed my first batch to ferment for 3 months and it tasted delicious. The next I opened after a few days already and it was equally good.

It is important to keep the water level above the cabbage or whatever veggies you are using. If that is not the case (as I experienced with one jar) the cabbage will turn grey and when you open it it will have a very unpleasant sour smell. Please discard and do not even sample if that is the case.

the kimchi version

The procedure is the same, the ingredients are as follows:

Daikon radish, burdock root, carrots, red radishes, horse radish, garlic, onions, red hot chilies, grated ginger root, leeks, scallions. All ingredients need to be grated or chopped. Some recipes call also for Jerusalem artichokes, turnips and burdock root.

4 final thoughts

It is, in my view, the duty of an apple to be crisp and crunchable, but a pear should have such a texture as leads to silent consumption. ~Edward Bunyard

goddess tara

For the longest time I have had a Green Tara sitting on the window sill in my bedroom. A friend gave it to me many years ago. A few months ago (just around the time when I started writing this book – coincidentally? - I decided to move her to the kitchen and then it occurred to me that the embodiment of the Mother energy that the Green Tara represents is exactly what the Earth needs: unconditional love, care and protection. It is said that she loves us so much that she has declared that she will remain in the Universe until all sentient beings have attained freedom. We have been taking from the Earth as our Mother for millennia; it is time to give back.

When the title and the idea of this book came to me I was not thinking about Tara, but now – as usually happens to me it all makes sense: I live GREEN, cook GREEN, eat GREEN and I love to GARDEN. I am surrounded by the gardens that I created over many years, by deep dark green forests and meadows and I even grow fruit trees and tomatoes in the house.

"Om Tara tuttare ture svaha"

"Om Tara tuttare ture svaha" is the mantra associated with the Goddess TARA. I chant it while I am in the garden and greenhouses to tend my plants and I chant it when I cook or prepare food.

It is also being said that Beings have been invoking Tara throughout the ages and that the immense accrued power of all those blessings comes through to anyone chanting the mantra with loving devotion today.

There are 21 different aspects of Tara. All can be invoked by chanting the heart mantra. Each of the 21 different aspects has its own mantra and color. Each form represents a different energy that addresses a specific issue.

I am focusing mostly on the Green Tara and the quality of enlightenment. "Om Tara tuttare ture svaha"; and of course on the White Tara representing healing, longevity, healthy lifestyle. "Om Tara tuttre ture mama ayuh punyajnana pushtu kuru svaha."

Tara, also means "star" or "she who ferries across," and she is a Bodhisattva of compassion who manifests in female form. In Tibetan, Tara is also known as "She Who Saves" by stepping from her lotus throne in order to help sentient beings.

Another striking thing about Tara is of course her greenness. She is represented as a beautiful, often voluptuous, sixteen-year-old woman, clad is silks and jewels: a highly attractive figure. And yet the color of her skin is green, and this surely clashes with her otherwise attractive appearance.

There is a beautiful painting at the Ma Shrine at Shoshoni retreat – one of my favorite places to go by myself or taking my students for a day of immersion into yogic lifestyle.

Tara is also associated with the element air, and she is considered a forest goddess. In one story she is shown as being clad in leaves. Her Pure Land is said to be lush and verdant, is covered with an abundance of trees and flowers; filled with the sound of many birds, and the murmur of waterfalls, creeks and brooks, enlivened with wild beasts of many kinds.

I live in the Colorado Rocky Mountains and the description of Tara matches my lifestyle perfectly, although at 9000 feet elevation it is not exactly "lush" and the climate is pretty harsh with superhot summer days, cool nights, torrential rains and long droughts; the winters can bring devastating winds, extreme snowstorms and bitter cold. Yet, there is so much green and beauty, pure air and pristine water still available and with my greenhouses, protected raised beds and cold frames as well as growing in the house I have created my own lush paradise. Maybe one day I will name my place "Green Tara Sanctuary"…

And now we are coming to the end of our Green Goddess Un/Cooking expedition together. There is no graduation ceremony. We will have to make our own ritual if we so desire, but I hope that rather making it one celebration you will continue your green, healthy journey for the rest of your life! I thank you for allowing me to be your guide and companion on this endeavor.

I encourage you to keep your healthy goals alive, daily! If you need support consider starting a health food or raw food group in your area or just join one of those wonderful meetup groups (http://www.meetup.com/) ; and you can always communicate with me as well. I would love to hear your stories. Here is a link to the blog on my website http://www.royalyogabailey.com/natural-healthyoga-blog.html .

However, I am confident that by now you will feel very comfortable with your new un/cooking and healthy/green living/eating practice and you will have established a habit of adding green/healthy foods on a regular basis. You will have benefited from your new experience; you have more energy, gave your immune system a boost, you got the GLOW!!!

What you are experiencing is personal growth towards well-being beyond your wildest dreams. You have stepped into the unknown and unfamiliar, you are getting more and more comfortable with foods that you would have not imagined could taste and make you feel THIS good. You might even feel more relaxed and at ease just because you are healthier and don't have all those aches and pains anymore. You probably lost weight or if your weight was perfect to begin with you might see a change in your skin tone right away, your skin might look more clear, younger and radiant. You may realize that you don't have allergies anymore! What a relief!

But you gave yourself permission to step onto and into a new life and path, you struggled, but you made it and emerged like a butterfly coming out of its cocoon. How do YOU feel now? Liberated? Light? Happy? Healthy? Ready to conquer anything? Ready to LOVE your life? Keep on going, it will get better and better every day!

I am sending you blessings of good health and happiness. May this book give you the support and ideas you need on your path to wellness.

OM NAMAH SHIVAYA

NAMASTE –

(The Divine in Me honors the Divine in YOU) a yogic greeting and blessing.

Bailey, Colorado – July 2012

"Health is a state of complete harmony of the body, mind and spirit. When one is free from physical disabilities and mental distractions, the gates of the soul open."
~B.K.S. Iyengar

Highly recommended books on yoga/meditation/mindfulness/journaling also written and published by the author.

Paul, Sophia S.; Journaling – *The Healing Journey.* **Bailey: Amazon.2012.**
ISBN-13: 978-1475075304 ; ISBN-10: 1475075308

Paul, Sophia S.; Yoga – *It's not about putting your foot behind your ear, an inspiring journey of transformation.* **Bailey: Amazon.2012.**
ISBN-13: 978-2475001317 ; ISBN-10: 2475001313

Paul, Sophia S.; *How to touch a Monk - FINDING OUR SACRED SPACE WITHIN.* **BAILEY: CREATE SPACE.** *2012.*ISBN -13:978-2475001317; ISBN-10- 2475001317

Paul, Sophia S.; *YOGA/Meditation - A COMPANION WORKBOOK TO* **"It's not about putting your foot behind your ear, an inspiring journey of transformation through YOGA". Bailey: Create Space. 2012.**
ISBN-13: 978-1475009637; ISBN-10: 1475009631

about the author

Sophia is a Doctor of Naturopathy, Cert. Yoga Instructor and Author. She specialized in Holistic Nutrition coaching along with Holistic/Natural Lifestyle changes to help YOU towards your goal of health and happiness in simple but very effective ways. This includes but is not limited to transition into

- vegetarianism/vegan/raw food
- treating/preventing diabetes naturally
- treating/preventing high cholesterol naturally
- healthy and lasting weight loss solutions
- ayurvedic assessments
- natural pain management
- holistic, natural gardening
- yoga/meditation coaching
- connecting with nature
- becoming your own therapist through journaling
- distant Reiki treatments
- .... you ask, I'll answer!!!

In "Green Goddess" she shares her favorite healthy recipes that are suited for diabetics and contain a variety of vegan/vegetarian/raw as well as cooked options. All are very simple, quick and easy to make.

Sophia lives a "Green Goddess Life" with her passion for gardening, healthy living and caring for the environment, yoga and meditation. She deeply loves nature, and resides in the magnificent Colorado Rocky Mountains.

www.royalyogabailey.com   www.amazon.com/author/sophiapaul

Made in the USA
San Bernardino, CA
07 August 2013